The Falklands War 1982 in Poetry

ANDY TRISH

Copyright © 2023 by Andy Trish

All rights reserved. No part of this book may be reproduced in any manner whatsoever without written permission except in the case of brief quotations embodied in critical articles and reviews.

First Printing, 2023

THE FALKLANDS WAR 1982
IN POETRY

In honour of my mother, Olive, who went through the pain of having both her sons in the Falklands War

Before delving into the pages of this book, I strongly recommend keeping a box of tissues within reach.

War is devoid of any semblance of amusement, and the contents within these chapters aim to shed light on the profound struggles endured by men, women, and children not just during the conflict but for years thereafter.

This compilation serves as a chronicle of my thoughts and emotions, originating from the time I first put pen to paper amidst the actual war. Now, 41 years later, I find myself presenting these reflections in print.

Within the narrative, the toll of 258 British lives lost during the conflict is acknowledged, a sombre count that extends to both civilians and military personnel, with many more perishing in the years that followed. Not every individual, battle, or vessel is named here, yet, as time unfolds, my collection expands. My aspiration is to eventually present a comprehensive account, honouring the fallen, so that together, we may pay tribute to their sacrifice. Andy Trish

Contents

Dedication   iv

1. Argentina Invades The Falkland Islands   1
2. At Sea   12
3. On Land And Air   42
4. Those Gone Before Us   61
5. Respite – The Wildlife   97
6. Mothers, Fathers, Brothers, Sisters, Wives, Girlfriends.   105
7. War Children   132
8. After The War   140
9. A Veteran Reminisces   158

About The Author   174

Chapter 1

Argentina Invades The Falkland Islands

On April 2, 1982, the Argentinian military Junta, under the leadership of General Leopoldo Galtieri, launched a sudden invasion of the Falkland Islands, seizing control of the capital, Stanley.

The incursion plunged the lives of men and women across the islands into disarray. Parents embarked on arduous journeys, navigating rough and impassable dirt tracks to retrieve their children from the boarding house in Stanley, realizing that their freedom was on the verge of being taken away.

In the face of this invasion, young men from both Britain and Argentina found themselves on the precipice of a conflict that would profoundly shape the trajectory of their lives. The impending war loomed large, with the ominous prospect that some would never return home.

Dark Clouds

In the South Atlantic breeze where the sea does roam,
A tranquil isle, our humble island home.
But now dark clouds have veiled our peaceful sky,
As strangers came with thunder, making angels cry.

Oh, Britannia, hear our desperate plea,
Your children stranded, yearning to be free.
It's 1982, the invaders come ashore,
Tears in our eyes, our voices raised in war.

The penguins march, their hearts heavy with woe,
As foreign flags on Falkland soil do grow.
Our cliffs, our bays, once touched by gentle hands,
Now bear the weight of an intruder's demands.

We call to you, with voices strong and clear,
Across the waves, may our cries reach your ear.
For in your embrace, we long to find,
The strength to reclaim what fate has maligned.

Oh, noble Lion, rise from your slumber,
To thwart the grip of this invader's plunder.
Bring forth the winds of freedom, wild and free,
To sweep away the chains from land and sea.

Let your mighty ships cut through the ocean's foam,
To bring salvation to our island home.
With courage in your heart and steel in your hand,
Restore the peace that graced this sacred land.

We stand united, resilient and bold,
Against the invaders, their tale must be told.
In your name, Britannia, we take our stand,
Liberate our shores, protect our island sand.

For in the heart of every islander's breast,
Beats a fervent hope, a prayer, a quest.
Oh, Britannia, in you we confide,
Guide us home with your strength, side by side.

The Conscript

In the land of youth, where dreams once thrived,
I walked home from school, alive and revived.
But fate's cruel hand, a sudden twist of time,
Thrust me into a world, untamed and unkind.

Approached by men with hardened gaze,
They declared my destiny, in a bewildering haze.
"No longer a boy, a soldier you shall be,
Defend our land, Islas Malvinas, from the enemy."

A van's cold embrace, whisked me away,
To an unknown place, where shadows held sway.
Uniform pressed upon my trembling frame,
A gun bestowed, with a weight of shame.

Set sail on a ship, with a heart burdened deep,
Crossing treacherous seas, where secrets we keep.
They spoke of British forces, marching fierce and bold,
On a desolate mountain, my destiny unfolds.

Mount Longdon, the sentinel of sorrow and woe,
Where bitter winds howled, and life's colours grew cold.
Stranded on its summit, in a barren abyss,
With scarce sustenance, and dreams dismissed.

Days blended like echoes, anguish etched on my face,
The hunger gnawed, my spirit embraced.
Amidst the frigid whispers of desolation's kiss,
I clutched my weapon, a symbol of darkness and bliss.

The enemy arrived, clad in foreign hue,
Stepping on sacred soil, where courage once grew.
Fear gripped my soul, but duty held tight,
To fire upon brothers, a relentless, grim plight.

In the chilling twilight, amidst cries and despair,
The battle roared, consuming the frigid air.
Yet deep within, a flicker of doubt,
Was this the path I truly sought out?

A reflection of innocence lost, in teary eyes,
Aching for solace beneath boundless skies.
Yearning for freedom, release from this plight,
To lay down arms, embrace the warmth of light.

For in the heart of conflict, amidst war's cruel decree,
A young Argentinian boy, yearning to be free.
In the midst of tragedy, compassion did bloom,
A testament to the human spirit, escaping the gloom.

Years have passed since those bitter days,
Yet memories linger, like echoes in a haze.
Let this poem serve, a reminder of strife,
And the cost of war, in a young boy's life.

An Islanders Thoughts

In the southern seas where the waves do roar,
A tale of islands, our home once more.
Falkland breezes, whispers in the air,
Now tainted by the shadow of despair.

On barren shores where sheep once grazed,
A foreign flag in the wind is raised.
Argentinian footsteps on sacred ground,
Our peaceful haven, now turmoil-bound.

In '82, the world held its breath,
As brothers fought on the edge of death.
Islanders caught in a geopolitical game,
Innocence lost, consumed by the flame.

Mountains echoed with the cries of the brave,
As invaders sought to enslave.
But in our hearts, resilience stirred,
A flame of hope that would not be deterred.

Huddled together, islander kin,
Facing a battle we never could win.
Yet in the face of an unwelcome fate,
We clung to our spirit, we stood straight.

The sea, our witness, turbulent and wild,
Whispered tales of a displaced child.
But in adversity, strength arose,
A resilient spirit that nobody knows.

Amidst the conflict, a longing for peace,
For wars to end, and tensions to cease.
A plea to the world, to stand in our stead,
To ease the pain and sorrow widespread.

Oh, Falkland Isles, though shadows loom,
Our spirit persists, dispelling the gloom.
In the heart of adversity, we'll find our way,
Reclaiming our haven, come what may.

Schools Out

It's time to go home, schools out at last.
As I glanced and saw, the grey van that passed.
four men got out, they came up to me,
Come on son, you are going to sea.

But my mum is waiting, she won't know where I am,
Sorry my friend, we don't give a damn.
You are coming with us, don't get smarmy,
All will be good, you are joining the Army.

I'm only 15, I tried to say
Not that they cared, they looked away.
In the van I was thrown, with more boys my age,
The doors slammed shut, we were trapped in that cage.

We were given a gun, no training to boot,
If you see any Brits, be sure to shoot.
On rocks up high, I was told to stay,
The English are coming, from far away.

They'll kill us and torture, fight and maim,
I really didn't want, to play this game.
The wind was so bitter, the snow so cold,
If we stayed here much longer, I wouldn't grow old.

Our homes in the hills, from hand we did carve,
Whilst the soldiers could eat, The conscripts would starve.
Then came the day, when bullets came flying,
And all around me, men were dying.

By luck, or chance, who would ever know,
I survived those days, and home I would go.
Those Islands are ours, So I've been told,
I really don't care, I'm out of the cold.

The Day Before We Sail

In the twilight's sombre embrace, we gather 'round,
A ship's crew reunited, adventure profound,
Called back from leave, duty's call in the air,
To sail for the Falklands, a battle to bear.

Tomorrow awaits us, the uncertain sea,
An odyssey of courage, destiny's decree,
With hearts intertwined, we embrace the night,
For it may be our last, ere dawn's first light.

The town awaits, alive with spirits high,
A fleeting respite, a chance to say goodbye,
In taverns we gather, as comrades we stand,
To toast to the future, our fate in the sand.

Cherished memories shared, like stars in the sky,
Bound by camaraderie, we stand tall and high,
Through laughter and tears, we forge bonds anew,
For the battles ahead, we'll see each other through.

Amidst the revelry, we treasure this time,
In the face of the unknown, we find solace in rhyme,
The clinking of glasses, a testament to life,
The camaraderie we share, a balm in the strife.

For tomorrow we sail, on a voyage unknown,
To a distant land where our bravery is shown,
But tonight we shall revel, without regret or sorrow,
And embrace every moment, as we forge our tomorrow.

In the morning's light, we'll bid the town adieu,
And set sail to the horizon, as the brave men we grew,
Though fate be uncertain, and perils abound,
Together we'll face it, till victory is found.

So, let us raise our glasses, and toast to the brave,
To the comrades we cherish, in this moment we save,
In the face of adversity, united we'll stand,
For we are the Royal Navy, a steadfast band.

From Homes Unknown

In a distant land, where the albatross fly,
A clash of lives, as history dared to defy.
Soldiers of fortune, in a war unforeseen,
Two worlds collided, in a merciless routine.

They came from afar, from homes unknown,
With dreams and hopes, each heart had sown.
Fathers, brothers, sons, and lovers too,
Bound by duty, they fought for what was true.

The Falklands, a battleground, where courage would unfold,
Where stories of valour and sacrifice were told.
In unfamiliar lands, where the winds did wail,
They marched in unison, facing the tempest's gale.

Behind the armour, beneath the weary eyes,
Were lives untold, where humanity lies.
They longed for home, for the touch of a hand,
In a world turned cold, they tried to withstand.

Mothers prayed and fathers wept,
As sons and daughters in battle slept.
In the hearts of comrades, bonds were forged in strife,
For in the crucible of war, they found a second life.

In the roar of cannons and the cries of pain,
They bore the weight of loss, like torrential rain.
Yet, in the midst of chaos, they found a kindred soul,
A brotherhood of warriors, whose stories make us whole.

They fought for freedom, for honour, for kin,
In the face of darkness, they chose to win.
And when the dust had settled, the battles ceased to roar,
They returned as heroes, forever changed by the war.

For those who fought and those they faced,
In the Falklands War, their destinies embraced.
In the pages of history, their legacy is inscribed,
A testament to human strength, where hope and love survived.

1982

In nineteen eighty-two, without a formal decree,
A storm of hostility brewed across the sea.
Britain's land was seized, its people in despair,
A violation of sovereignty, an act so unfair.

The drums of war resounded with a thunderous roar,
As soldiers, sailors, and airmen marched toward the shore.
Their purpose was unwavering, united they had stood,
Determined to reclaim what had been taken for good.

The sea turned crimson, tinged with sorrow and pain,
As brave hearts fell, forever etched in the terrain.
Two-hundred and fifty-eight, British lives lost,
Their sacrifice should never be forgotten or tossed.

But let us not forget, for on the other side,
Lay Argentinian sons, men who also died.
More lives consumed by the flames of war,
Their losses, too, a tragedy we should deplore.

The term "conflict" may downplay the scenes that unfurled,
But in truth, it was a war that shook the world.
A clash of nations, a fight for pride and land,
Where many paid the price with a scarred, wounded hand.

So let us remember the fallen, regardless of their name,
And recognize the truth, lest we forget their claim.
The Falklands War, a chapter etched in history's tome,
Where lives were lost, and nations yearned for home.

I Don't Know

Tell us where they are, or your husband will soon be dead,
Tell us now, tell us fast, (gun pointed at my husbands head).
My children crying, shaking like mad,
As the Argentinians were going to murder their dad.

I don't know, I don't know, from my mouth I lied,
I have no idea where, the special forces hide.
They didn't believe me, I'll always know,
But they did eventually let him go.

We will look and we'll find them and if we do,
We'll be back to deal with all of you.
No words can describe, just how I felt,
As they walked off in the distance, gun in it's belt.

We cuddled, we cried, for as long as we live,
I knew then this was something I could never forgive.
The soldiers and sailors, airmen who came,
Gave us hope in our future, putting the Argies to shame.

Chapter 2

At Sea

A formidable fleet consisting of 127 ships and submarines from the Royal and Merchant Navy, encompassing cargo vessels, tankers, and cruise liners, vividly illustrates the extensive logistical and military endeavours spearheaded by the United Kingdom. This diverse array of ships underwent strategic adaptations to fulfill various roles, underscoring the multifaceted nature of the military operation.

The average age of Royal Naval personnel in the Falklands War was 23.

The crews aboard the requisitioned ships, initially engaged in civilian pursuits, were abruptly thrust into pivotal roles within a major military operation. Their capacity to swiftly adapt to the demands of wartime service stands as a testament to the flexibility and resilience inherent in both military and civilian personnel involved in the Falklands War.

I am the sea

I am the sea, the ancient, the wide,
Witness to time, with nowhere to hide.
In my depths, secrets lie,
Under the watchful, endless sky.

Came they once, with steel and smoke,
Upon my surface, the war awoke.
Ships of iron, hearts of stone,
In my waters, their fates were sewn.

I cradled them, in my icy hold,
Watched the young and the brave, the bold.
Heard their cries, their whispered prayers,
As they danced with death, unawares.

The sky turned red, the air aflame,
In my depths, they called my name.
Into my arms, they sank to rest,
The fallen warriors, on my chest.

I washed their wounds, I soothed their pain,
In the endless cycle, of war's refrain.
Yet, I am the sea, I do not judge,
I only embrace, I do not begrudge.

Now, all is calm, the war is past,
Only echoes remain, of the blast.
I am the sea, the ancient, the wide,
The keeper of secrets, where truths reside.

In my depths, the stories sleep,
Of the Falklands War, where sorrows seep.
I am the sea, the silent witness,
To mankind's dance, with death's abyss.

Santa Fe

In the frozen depths of South Georgia's land,
Where heroes tread on icy terrain so grand,
Amidst the Falklands' war, a mission arose,
A tale of bravery that forever glows.

The ARA Santa Fe, an Argentine foe,
A grounded threat, poised to strike a blow,
But British resolve would not be undone,
A Special Forces mission had just begun.

Through snow and ice, the SBS did tread,
With hearts of stone, no fear in their stead,
Led by Major Delves, a pillar of might,
They ventured forth, a fearless sight.

Their steps, like whispers upon frozen ground,
Silent shadows amidst the night profound,
With skillful precision, they closed the gap,
To infiltrate the vessel's frozen trap.

Against the odds, they breached the hull,
In stealth, they ventured, their hearts full,
Amidst the Santa Fe's dim-lit domain,
They sought to seize victory, without disdain.

Through winding corridors, danger they met,
The Argentine sailors, a foe they had to get,
With courage aflame, they pressed ahead,
For the mission's success, they steadfastly bled.

Explosions erupted, chaos did ignite,
Yet undeterred, they fought through the night,
Though setback struck, their spirit held true,
They gathered intel, a vital breakthrough.

The codes and charts, the secrets they sought,
From the enemy's grasp, they had been caught,
With triumph and purpose, they made their retreat,
Their heroic mission, now bittersweet.

So let us remember those heroes of yore,
Whose bravery and spirit we forever adore,
In the pages of history, their story we tell,
Of the Falklands' heroes, who fought and fell.

The Lady Elizabeth

Upon the harbour, quiet and still,
Rests Lady Elizabeth, wrought of steel.
Her form a shadow in Falkland's mist,
A spectral relic, by time's hand kissed.

She lies in Stanley's tender care,
A tale of ancient journeys bare,
A vessel forged in fire and strife,
Now anchored to a second life.

In her holds, the whispers sound,
Of tempests braved, in lore profound.
Once she danced on Neptune's palm,
Survived his anger, his eerie calm.

Then came the Falklands, shrouded in war,
Her deck again trod, as in days of yore.
The SBS, silent as night,
Boarded her hull in the ghostly light.

Through her veins, they moved unseen,
On a mission covert, sharp and keen.
With Argentinian eyes nearby,
Under a moonless, starless sky.

Echoes of footfall on her spine,
The old ship hummed, in clandestine.
A silent sentinel, stout and brave,
In her heart, secrets safely stowed away.

The night was tense, the air was cold,
As whispered stories began to unfold.
She stood her ground, through the ordeal,
The Elizabeth, the silent seal.

Now she slumbers in Stanley's hold,
Her tales untold, yet deeply sowed.
A phantom of history, stoic, grand,
An unsung hero in Falkland's sand.

Remember the Lady, the vessel, the site,
Where shadows danced in the pallid light.
In war's harsh song, and peace's hum,
She serves as testament, silent and numb.

HMS Sheffield

In the southern seas where shadows crawl,
A tale of darkness, of a ship's cruel fall.
HMS Sheffield, proud and bold,
In the Falklands War, a story to be told.

Beneath the moon, on silent waves,
The whispers of war, like ocean graves.
A dance of death, in the cold night air,
As fate descended with a sinister glare.

The South Atlantic, a desolate stage,
Where tragedy wrote its haunting page.
HMS Sheffield, a steel behemoth,
In the grip of war's relentless scythe.

The enemy lurked in the ocean's shroud,
A deadly silence, a ghostly crowd.
Then came the strike, a fiery lance,
A cruel twist in war's macabre dance.

Explosions echoed through the naval abyss,
As flames engulfed the vessel in a deadly kiss.
The heart of the ship, now a funeral pyre,
A sombre requiem, a funeral choir.

Men trapped in the metal jaws of despair,
Their voices lost in the ocean's cold stare.
The sea, witness to the tragedy unfold,
As the story of Sheffield in darkness is told.

Smoke and sorrow veiled the moonlit night,
A spectre of loss, a chilling sight.
The ship once proud, now a watery tomb,
In the depths of sorrow, in the cold and gloom.

The Navy wept, the ocean sighed,
As the echoes of war in the waters died.
HMS Sheffield, a name engraved in sorrow,
A haunting tale of a ship's dark tomorrow.

HMS Ardent

In the South Atlantic's expanse of blue,
Where winds whisper tales both brave and true,
A saga unfolds 'neath the Falklands sky,
Of HMS Ardent, with courage held high.

Through waves that roared with a tempest's might,
She sailed with purpose, through day and night.
A vessel of steel, a heart of the bold,
In the Falklands War, her story told.

Upon the horizon, a conflict brewed,
Nations clashed, and heroes ensued.
Ardent, a guardian in the ocean's vast,
A sentinel ship in a drama cast.

Amidst the splendour of the southern light,
Ardent faced a relentless, daunting fight.
Against the Argentine forces she stood,
In the name of freedom, for the common good.

On waves of battle, she danced with grace,
Defying peril in that distant place.
Her crew, a brotherhood bound by the sea,
Fighting for honour, for victory.

Ardent, a flame in the naval array,
In Falklands' waters, where shadows lay.
Bravery etched in each sailor's gaze,
A testament to those tumultuous days.

In the crucible of war, she took her stand,
Ardent, resolute in the Falklands' sand.
Against the tempest of conflict's roar,
She sailed with valour, forevermore.

Yet, in the echoes of the Southern Cross,
Ardent's sacrifice was not a loss.
For in the stories of naval lore,
Her spirit lives on forevermore.

In the hallowed waves where history's spun,
HMS Ardent, under the Falklands sun,
A chapter written, a tale to impart,
Of bravery, sacrifice, and a ship's brave heart.

HMS Antelope

In Falkland's solemn waters, 'neath the vast and endless sky,
Where the winds of fate did gather, and the tears of loved ones lie,
I gaze upon the marker buoy, above the ship so brave,
HMS Antelope, forever resting in her watery grave.

In Bomb Alley's treacherous embrace, she sailed with valour true,
Her crew, courageous souls, they faced the enemy, they knew,
That in this battle's fiery storm, where dangers did amass,
Their sacrifice would echo through time, a solemn looking glass.

Oh, HMS Antelope, noble ship of iron might,
Through tumultuous seas you sailed, into the darkest night,
Your sailors, brave and steadfast, on that fateful day they fell,
Their stories etched in history, their memories we shall tell.

As waves of sorrow wash ashore, hearts heavy with despair,
We remember those who served on you, in the Falklands' frigid air,
For in the face of adversity, they stood, unwavering and bold,
Their spirits live on in the stories told.

With every crashing wave that breaks, with every seagull's cry,
We honour your memory, HMS Antelope, as time goes by,
In Bomb Alley's haunting waters, where your final journey lay,
We remember the lives lost, and the price they had to pay.

Oh, let us not forget the cost, the sacrifice they made,
As we stand here on this shoreline, in the shadows of your shade,
HMS Antelope, you rest beneath the ocean's endless blue,
But your legacy and bravery shine, a beacon for us to renew.

In the Falkland Islands' solemn waters, where memories persist,
We pay our respects to you, dear ship, and those you dearly missed,
In the quiet of this moment, as we gaze upon the sea,
We remember, honour, and cherish, the lives that went with thee.

Bomb Alley

In Bomb Alley's shadowed depths they stood,
Upon the waves of sorrow's flood,
Brave souls who sailed to meet their fate,
In Falklands' hell, where death did wait.

The battle raged on rocky shores,
Where life's frail thread was torn in wars,
In skies of fire, blackened smoke,
The price of freedom, life bespoke.

San Carlos waters, cold as ice,
Bore witness to the sacrifice,
As ships ablaze and spirits broke,
Amidst the chaos, courage spoke.

A dance of darkness, death's embrace,
In Bomb Alley's haunting grace,
The echoes of each cannon's roar,
Still resonate along that shore.

The crimson sea, a gruesome sight,
A canvas painted in the night,
With shattered dreams and broken pride,
In Falklands' heart, where many died.

The cries of pain, the silent screams,
Still linger in the midnight dreams,
The fallen heroes, lost and brave,
Now rest forever in a watery grave.

And though the battle's dust has cleared,
The memory's mark will not be sheared,
In Bomb Alley's depths so deep,
The cost of war, forever weep.

Atlantic Conveyor

In the depths of sorrow's dark embrace,
A tale unfolded, etched with grace,
Amidst the tempest's relentless roar,
The Atlantic Conveyor met a fateful shore.

In '82, a year of strife,
In Falklands' conflict, warriors strive,
Amidst the chaos, amidst the fight,
A ship emerged, a guiding light.

The Conveyor sailed with steadfast will,
Her cargo precious, a nation's thrill,
Amidst her decks, hopes took flight,
A lifeline woven, in darkest night.

Through treacherous seas, she forged her way,
Unyielding spirit, undeterred, she'd sway,
Braving the tempest, her crew stood tall,
Their courage unmatched, united, they'd call.

But fate, relentless, had other plans,
A missile's cruel strike, like fiery brands,
A thunderous blow, a piercing cry,
The Conveyor's fate, now sealed, goodbye.

Twelve lives lost, their essence untold,
In the ocean's depths, their stories unfold,
Their sacrifice, a haunting refrain,
Etched in the hearts, in memory's domain.

Oh, the anguish, the grief that day,
When loved ones wept, and skies turned grey,
Yet amidst the sorrow, a flicker of light,
Their spirits endure, shining bright.

For in the annals of the heroes tale,
Their legacy, a triumphant sail,
Their courage lives on, forevermore,
In the souls they touched, in hearts they bore.

We remember them, those heroes true,
Their sacrifice, a debt we owe, too,
On the Atlantic Conveyor's hallowed ground,
Their spirits soar, with love profound.

Sir Tristram

In the misty dawn of April's tender bloom,
From Belize, Sir Tristram was called to assume,
A venture great, Operation Corporate's boon,
To retake Falklands beneath the southern moon.

Bearing men and might across the ocean's vast,
Into Fitzroy Cove, it anchored at last.
Then, from Argentine skies, the die was cast,
Skyhawks struck hard, flying so fast.

Decks were strafed, two brave souls found their doom,
A bomb through the deck, a looming tomb.
But the fuse was slow, giving time to exhume,
The living from death, in the gathering gloom.

Abandoned and scarred, yet not succumbing,
Served as home for the 97th, their hearts drumming.
In Port Stanley's bosom, her story still humming,
A wounded guardian, fate's harsh strumming.

Yet from ashes and ruin, like the mythical bird,
To Stanley she sailed, her purpose not blurred.
Rebuilt and reborn, her spirit unstirred,
In '85 returned, her duty conferred.

In the Gulf's heated blaze, the Balkans' raw sore,
Delivering relief when storms did roar,
In Sierra Leone's plight, and Iraq's war,
Sir Tristram sailed on, adding to her lore.

Finally at rest in two thousand and five,
Yet even in slumber, her legacy thrives,
Training Special Forces, her spirit survives,
In the heart of the Fleet, Sir Tristram yet strives.

A Bomb Unbinds

In the skies above, a deadly fate unwinds,
From the Argentine skies, I'm a bomb that unbinds.
In the Falklands' turmoil, amidst the fray,
Towards Sir Tristram, I descend today.

A vessel strong, adorned in Union Jack,
A Royal Navy ship, steadfast in attack.
Two sailors below, their hearts intertwined,
Bound by duty, and the sea's relentless grind.

Through the wailing winds, I plummet low,
A harbinger of sorrow, an imminent blow.
But let me pause, a moment, if I may,
To contemplate the cost of this dire day.

In war's cruel grip, we're all but pawns,
No choice in the battles we're drawn upon.
Yet in these last moments, my mind does dwell,
On the souls below, a tale to tell.

Two men, like brothers, in the face of strife,
Bracing for the impact that will claim their life.
Their laughter and tears, their dreams and fears,
All suspended now, as the end appears.

Beyond the flags, the politics, and divide,
Lay human hearts, beating deep inside.
Fathers, brothers, sons, they leave behind,
Aching hearts, as fate becomes unkind.

To those below, I beg your grace,
As I approach this sombre place.
May you find solace in love's embrace,
As I'm but a vessel, in this sombre space.

For the horrors of war, I cannot abate,
Yet in these final seconds, let us contemplate,
The price of conflict, the lives it takes,
And strive for a world where peace awakes.

The sea of tears, in oceans wide,
Should beckon us to turn the tide.
To build a world where all can thrive,
And no more bombs or lives deprived.

As I reach my destination's shore,
I beseech humanity to explore,
Paths of understanding, compassion, and more,
For in unity, we can truly soar.

May my destruction not be in vain,
But a reminder of the souls in pain.
In this poem's echo, let us reclaim,
A world of peace, where love will reign.

A Rainbow Over The Fallen

In Fitzroy's cold and tumultuous embrace,
Where roaring waves conceal a sombre grace,
Two noble ships, Sir Galahad and Tristram, sailed,
Their fates entwined, by cruel war impaled.

A rainbow over the fallen, arched so high,
Its colours wept, as brave souls kissed the sky.
Upon those decks, valiant hearts beat strong,
Bound for battle, amid the strife so wrong.

Sir Galahad, a vessel of hope and might,
Carried warriors fierce, in the heat of the fight.
Yet fate's cruel hand did intervene,
And tragedy reigned, the decks turned mean.

Sir Tristram, companion to the Galahad's quest,
In those dark waters, fate's verdict pressed.
The sea turned crimson, a sorrowful hue,
As lives were shattered, hearts pierced through.

A rainbow over the fallen, in tears did gleam,
A fragile bridge between life's fleeting dream,
The hues reflected the souls that took flight,
Amidst the chaos and the unforgiving night.

Brothers and sisters, comrades so true,
In Fitzroy's waters, your courage grew.
Though darkness claimed you, your light remains,
A rainbow's promise through sorrows and pains.

So let us remember, the fallen so dear,
Their sacrifices profound, crystal clear.
May their memory be a beacon of light,
Guiding us through darkness, in the blackest night.

A rainbow over the fallen, forever to shine,
A tribute to those who paid freedom's fine.
In Fitzroy's embrace, where tears and sea blend,
Their courage and sacrifice, we shall defend.

Burning Flames

> The flames in your eyes,
> Only I could see.
> A reflection so scary,
> As you looked at me.
>
> My skin, it was melting,
> Under clothes as they burned.
> But as bad as it was,
> Your head never turned.
>
> Reassurance you gave,
> All would be good.
> The fire was subsiding,
> Right where I stood.
>
> The ship was but sinking,
> Still did you stay.
> There by my side,
> As the sky turned grey.

They hoisted us up,
On a winch over sea.
My skin it was melting,
But you were with me.

My children, my family,
My lovely wife.
Will always be grateful,
You saved my life.

Whilst the scars they did heal,
And the pain did subside.
I still see the flames burning,
In every inch of my mind.

HMS Glamorgan

In the shadow of the Southern Cross we stand,
Before the Glamorgan memorial, on this solemn land.
Names etched in stone, a tribute to the brave,
Who in '82's conflict, found a watery grave.

Poppies and crosses, tokens of the heart,
Left by fellow veterans, a solemn, sacred art.
They traveled here to honour and to mourn,
In this distant place where heroes were born.

Beyond the memorial, the endless sea does call,
As memories of war like ghosts, begin to fall.
Those days of conflict, the battles fierce and wild,
Each wave a reminder of a brave seafarer's child.

Families and friends, they left behind,
In their hearts, a void, a love forever enshrined.
We think of their sacrifice, their courage unmeasured,
And the bonds of unity that war's fire has treasured.

Proud men and women, with hands and hearts so skilled,
Built this monument, their purpose fulfilled.
A testament of love, respect, and grace,
For those who gave all in this far-off place.

In the Falkland Islands, under the endless sky,
We remember the fallen, with a tear in our eye.
Their legacy lives on in the wind and the sea,
In this hallowed place, where heroes will always be.

Gone Forever

I stood on deck,
words were said.
heads bowed,
in front, the dead.

these men, unknown,
to you and me.
but comrades lost,
slipped, into the sea.

gone forever,
before loved ones told.
young men whose bodies,
will never grow old.

Each day this happened,
My heart strings tore.
These men were lost,
In the Falklands War.

As The Sun Sets Low

As the sun dips low o'er the seashore's edge,
A solemn moment, we must now pledge,
To remember those lost, the brave and the free,
In the Falklands War, by the vast, unforgiving sea.

Beneath the golden hues of the setting sun,
Courageous hearts fought, their battles begun,
Amidst the waves' fury and the bitter cold,
Their stories of loss, forever told.

In the South Atlantic's tempestuous embrace,
A conflict unfolded in a desolate space,
Sailors and soldiers, their lives on the line,
For their homeland's honour, they did shine.

The sea, a relentless and formidable foe,
Took some from us, where the wild winds blow,
But in our hearts, their memory remains,
Their sacrifice not lost, in history's chains.

Let us not forget those who served with pride,
On both sides of the conflict, on that turbulent tide,
For in remembrance, we find the way,
To honour the fallen, and their bravery display.

As the sun sets low o'er the seashore's crest,
In our thoughts and prayers, they shall forever rest,
The souls who journeyed to the unknown deep,
In the Falklands War, their watch we shall keep.

Thank you

In days of old, when winds did howl,
And tempests roared on ocean's scowl,
To Falklands' shores, we sailed afar,
A brave mission, guided by a shining star.

Through raging seas, we fought the storm,
But not alone, for hearts were warm,
The Merchant Navy, and RFA's pride,
With courage unmatched, stood by our side.

Civilians bold, with hearts of steel,
Answered the call, to fight and heal,
They volunteered, without a pause,
To share the burden, uphold the cause.

Amidst the chaos, they brought us aid,
Their selfless service, no debt repaid,
With every sunrise, hope would gleam,
Because of them, we dared to dream.

In battle's fury, they faced the dread,
With steadfast honour, they bravely tread,
civilian ships, a lifeline's grace,
Amidst the perilous, tumultuous space.

With each supply, their hearts they'd pour,
Unyielding, as waves crashed on the shore,
Their hands, a lifeline, a beacon bright,
Guiding us through the darkest night.

To you, dear civilians, our voices raise,
In heartfelt gratitude, we sing your praise,
For in our triumphs, your part was vast,
In every memory, your names are cast.

Though years have passed, our hearts still know,
The debt we owe, the love we sow,
To the Merchant Navy, and RFA's might,
You are forever, our guiding light.

So, let us celebrate the brave and true,
The civilian heroes, who joined our crew,
For in their valour, courage, and grace,
The spirit of the Falklands War we embrace.

The Oceans Deep

Oh, boundless ocean, enigmatic and grand,
A vast area of wonders, where secrets expand,
Your power unfathomable, your depths unknown,
In your shifting moods, your majesty is shown.

Upon your large canvas, the sun paints its hues,
Golden dawn and twilight's purples infuse,
Your waves dance with grace, in rhythmic flow,
A symphony of tides, a ballet to bestow.

Beneath the azure veil, a world concealed,
A myriad of life forms, their fate unsealed,
From smallest creatures to the giants unknown,
In hidden realms, life's miracles are sown.

Yet, your might is not confined to gentle grace,
You unleash tempests, a furious embrace,
With roiling waves and thunderous roars,
You remind us mortals of your unyielding force.

Amidst your vast expanse, a fleet takes flight,
To Falkland Islands, where history did ignite,
In the tempest of battle, on distant shores,
Ships carried warriors, off to the wars.

Their hearts were bound with courage and fear,
On your vast bosom, they shed a warrior's tear,
Amidst the fights, the bloodshed, and pain,
You carried their hopes, and their dreams did sustain.

Though your depths conceal the scars of strife,
The Falklands War, a chapter of human life,
Yet even amid conflict, a lesson is clear,
The unity of nations, compassion held dear.

Oh, ocean, eternal, in your embrace,
Countless stories, legends, you interlace,
From whispered secrets to the grandest tale,
You cradle them all, without judgment or scale.

HMS Hermes

In the heart of the storm, on the deck I stand,
A guardian of the sky, a vigilant hand.
HMS Hermes, our mighty ship of pride,
To the Falklands we sail, side by side.

Above me, the heavens, dark and unforgiving,
A battle of wills, where fate is unwritten.
As Seakings take flight, with blades slicing the air,
And Sea Harriers soar, in their might, they dare.

I watch them ascend, blades going round,
Praying they'll return, safe and sound.
For they are our heroes, the brave and the bold,
Whose stories untold, in history unfold.

Their wings carry hopes, dreams, and fears,
As they pierce through the clouds, leaving trails of tears.
Each mission they undertake, a perilous flight,
To defend our freedom, with all their might.

Through treacherous skies, they navigate,
Guided by courage, in their hearts innate.
Their mission, a purpose, to protect and to save,
For their comrades on land, they're ever so brave.

In the face of danger, they stand undeterred,
Their spirits unyielding, their hearts never blurred.
Through fire and smoke, they press on with might,
To bring back our warriors, in the darkest of night.

Oh, how I pray, as they vanish from sight,
That they'll return safely, success in their fight.
Their names etched in memory, their valour renowned,
As they touch down on Hermes, solid ground.

In the aftermath, as the battle subsides,
We gather the fallen, with tears in our eyes.
For some never made it back to our shore,
Their sacrifice honoured, forevermore.

So, here on the flight deck, where dreams take flight,
We bow our heads, and we pray each night.
For the Seakings and Harriers, gallant and true,
May God protect them, as they see us through.

In the crucible of war, we find our resolve,
On HMS Hermes, we steadfastly evolve.
And as we sail home, under a crimson sky,
We remember the fallen, with a tear in our eye.

From the sea – Freedom

From the sea's embrace, a call to rise,
A distant cry, a land to prize.
In battles fierce, where courage thrives,
The Falklands stand, where freedom strives.

Amidst the waves, a storm unleashed,
Nations clashed, their wills reached.
Islands coveted, a conflict born,
Yet within the tempest, hope was sworn.

Across the ocean, a distant land,
Brave souls sailed, to take a stand.
Their purpose clear, their hearts ablaze,
Defending home in foreign haze.

From the sea they came, a force untamed,
United soldiers, honour proclaimed.
A canvas vast, painted with strife,
Their valiant steps, etching life.

With every footfall, echoes of might,
Resolute souls, day and night.
They faced the tempest, undeterred,
For freedom's sake, their voices stirred.

In battles fierce, they forged ahead,
The fallen mourned, their spirits spread.
Through smoke and fire, they stood tall,
Answering the sea's defiant call.

From the sea - Freedom, a bond revealed,
The Falklands etched, a battlefield.
A testament to resolve and might,
Their sacrifice, a formidable sight.

And as the sea now whispers low,
Their story lives, an eternal glow.
From the sea they came, freedom's plea,
The Falklands War, a legacy.

I Wish It Was Me

In the shadowed depths of the vast, cruel sea,
Lies a sailor, silent, where he was meant to be.
The waves whisper tales of strength and might,
Of a war that consumed, and a fateful night.

His friend stands ashore, eyes misted with grief,
Haunted by memories, seeking relief.
The wind carries echoes of battles long past,
Of aircraft and gunfire, and a friendship that'd last.

They sailed side by side, through tempests and calm,
Brothers in spirit, with a seafarer's psalm.
But war, with its fury, tore them apart,
One claimed by the ocean, one with a broken heart.

The survivor's soul, heavy with guilt and despair,
Wanders the shores, gasping for air.
For every horizon, every crest of a wave,
Brings visions of his friend, whom he couldn't save.

"I wish it was me," he murmurs to the breeze,
As he kneels on the sand, brought to his knees.
For in the cruel dance of bullets and fate,
He was left behind, with a heart full of hate.

The moon casts a glow on the shimmering tide,
As he thinks of the day his comrade died.
The weight of survival, a burden so deep,
Pulls at his heart, as he weeps.

In dreams, they meet on some distant shore,
Where war is a memory, pain is no more.
But until that day, he's bound to the sea,
Whispering, "I wish, oh I wish, it was me."

The Skin I Live In

In the heart of the raging storm, I stood,
A sailor's soul, on seas of fire and blood,
Amidst the Falklands' fateful clash,
Where destiny's cruel hand did crash.

Flames embraced me, a wicked dance,
Devouring flesh in a deadly trance,
The ship became a charred old mess,
A battleground of pain to excess.

The skin I live in, now a tapestry of pain,
Charred remnants of life, forever stained,
Flesh and memory fused in agony's art,
A symphony of scars etched on my heart.

In the darkness of the ship's embrace,
I met the agony of fire's cruel grace,
The burnished agony, searing deep,
A silent scream, a secret I keep.

The skin I live in, a canvas of despair,
A monument to anguish, a silent prayer,
I wear my scars like armour, bold,
A tale untold, of battles fought and souls sold.

Amidst the shadows, I find my way,
Haunted by the echoes of that fateful day,
The skin I live in, a testament to strife,
A survivor's tale etched in the fabric of life.

The scars that mar, the pain that's real,
A reminder of wounds time cannot heal,
Yet in the depths of darkness, I find my light,
For within this skin, I claim my might.

So let the world see my scars, my pain,
For they're the emblem of battles won in vain,
The skin I live in, a story of strength,
A journey through fire's relentless length.

Conquerors Silence

In the depths of the sea, I lie,
A vessel of death 'neath the stormy sky.
Cold metal heart, devoid of remorse,
A harbinger of doom, on a deadly course.

Through murky waters, I silently glide,
A phantom of dread, lurking 'neath the tide.
Thoughts swirl like shadows in this hollow tomb,
As I approach the target of impending doom.

Belgrano, a name etched in history's pain,
A ship bound for doom, in the fateful rain.
Men aboard, unaware of their fate,
Innocence betrayed by the hand of hate.

A decision made, a button to press,
To unleash destruction, chaos, distress.
The weight of the world, heavy on my soul,
As I bear witness to lives being stole.

In the silence of this submerged domain,
I grapple with guilt, a heart heavy with pain.
Does duty demand such a sinister toll?
To snuff out existence, the price of control.

The echoes of conscience reverberate deep,
A haunting reminder of promises to keep.
Dark waters mirror the depths of my soul,
As I become a vessel for death to unroll.

Beneath the stars that refuse to shine,
I ponder the nature of humanity's line.
In this submarine's depths, a soul left to rot,
Haunted by the choices that cannot be forgot.

Chapter 3

On Land And Air

The rough terrain and weather at the time of the war in the Falkland Islands proved extremely challenging for the land and air forces. The weight of the kit alone that had to be transported by foot for many miles across treacherous landscapes showed true strength. Young men, some barely out of training fighting alongside seasoned veterans. I bow my head to all who fought on these lands.

Falkland Islands Defence Force

In '82, on April's first day,
Falkland's fate hung in the fray.
With courage stout and hearts ablaze,
FIDF stood, their island's praise.

In remote settlements they dwelled,
With notice scarce, their ranks propelled.
From 120, thirty-two did rise,
To face the threat from foreign skies.

Sir Rex Hunt, a leader bold,
Ordered surrender, stories told,
Yet hearts undaunted, spirits free,
Falkland's sons refused to flee.

Argentines came, equipment seized,
Declared them outlaws, hearts unpleased.
Under house arrest, they bore the weight,
Till freedom dawned, a rightful fate.

Terry Peck, a hero's name,
Spied and fought in Freedom's flame.
With Parachute Regiment, he stood,
At Mount Longdon, in brotherhood.

In 2021, a motto gained,
"Faithful in Defence," proclaimed.
By the Queen's grace, they earned their name,
In history's annals, etched in fame.

Through trials endured, and battles fought,
Falkland's spirit, cannot be bought.
Faithful in Defence, their guiding star,
Guardians of home, no matter how far.

The Battle For Goose Green

In the heart of night, where shadows creep,
The battle drums of Goose Green beat,
A field of death, where souls entwine,
As darkness weaves its web malign.

Soldiers clad in raven's cloak,
Marched into chaos, fate bespoke,
Their breaths like mist in moonlit haze,
In this forsaken, blood-soaked maze.

The moon concealed its face in dread,
As life and hope were left for dead,
The cries of anguish pierced the air,
A symphony of torment, despair.

Bullets gleamed with icy fire,
Innocence consumed by war's dire,
A dance of doom, a deadly trance,
As blood was shed with brutal chance.

The earth itself cried out in pain,
Absorbing secrets, each crimson stain,
Grim echoes of a desperate plea,
For peace to reign, for hearts to see.

But on it raged, the battle's fire,
A symphony of violence and ire,
Where life was marked for sacrifice,
And hope was swallowed by the night.

At last, the dawn began to break,
Revealing the toll that war did make,
The field lay littered, souls departed,
A landscape scarred and broken-hearted.

The battle for Goose Green, a tale untold,
Of lives and dreams forever stole,
In darkness fought, in darkness won,
A stark reminder of what's done.

So let us pause and never forget,
The price of war, the lives beset,
In Goose Green's name, let's strive to find,
A world where peace and light align.

Goose Green

The sun shines low upon the plain,
And darkness gathers in the west;
The sheep are folded in their pen,
The cattle rest, wool on their chest.

But still the sentries watch and wait,
Their rifles ready in their hands;
For who can tell when foemen may
Steal forth to ravage field and lands.

The night is dark, the night is still,
The stars shine brightly overhead;
The only sound is that of feet
That tread the dewy grass instead.

They come, they come! The foemen come!
The battle-cry is heard afar;
The rifles ring, the bullets fly,
And many a brave man falls to die.

But still the gallant British stand,
And still they fight with courage true;
And soon the foemen turn and fly,
And leave the field to British view.

The victory is ours at last,
And Goose Green is ours again;
And we shall never rest content
Until the whole of Britain's reign

Is safe from foreign foemen's hand,
And all her children live in peace;
Then shall we sing with joyful heart,
"God save the Queen!" and raise our voice.

In praise of Him who gave us strength
To win this glorious victory,
And who will guard us still from harm
In all our days of life to be.

It Only Took Seconds.

It only took seconds,
It didn't take much.
The landmine went off,
At the slightest touch.

My body went flying,
Bits everywhere.
Really? What's happening,
Why's my leg over there.

Looking down as I dared,
And what did I see.
What looked like red jelly,
nothing below the knee.

I just couldn't fathom,
What was happening at all.
I lifted my arm up,
No hand at all.

The screams and the shouting,
Man down just ahead.
Don't go any further,
We don't want you dead.

Then came the peace,
Right after that shout.
My mind couldn't take it,
I had just blacked out.

A Bullet Waits

Through the barrel's dark and narrow lane,
A bullet waits, its purpose set aflame.
Bound for war, it yearns to take flight,
To pierce the shadows, embrace the fight.

The trigger pulled, a thunderous sound,
The bullet soars, breaking free from the ground.
A streak of silver in the cold, cruel air,
It seeks its mark, with deadly flair.

Swiftly it cuts through the battlefield's haze,
A messenger of fate in this brutal maze.
Through shattered hopes and shattered dreams,
It races onward, fuelled by war's screams.

No conscience or mercy guides its path,
A cold-hearted messenger, harbinger of wrath.
It cares not for sides or the reason behind,
Its purpose singular, to strike, unbind.

With lethal precision, it surges ahead,
Through chaos and fear, its presence spread.
The world blurs past, a fleeting scene,
As the bullet hurtles toward its unforeseen.

In the face of danger, it knows no fear,
As death draws closer, its mission near.
It whispers secrets of the lives it's claimed,
Of destinies altered, forever maimed.

And in that moment, as it finds its mark,
The battlefield trembles, plunged into the dark.
A life extinguished, a story untold,
As the bullet's tale continues to unfold.

But beyond the smoke and the shattered bone,
A bullet's journey is not its own.
In the echoes of war, a plea to be heard,
To ponder the cost of each vengeful word.

For in the barrel's grip, a truth prevails,
That bullets cannot mend the world's torn veils.
It's in our hands, in the choices we make,
To seek peace and harmony, for humanity's sake.

So let us reflect on this bullet's flight,
And strive to end the perpetual night.
For in the end, it's not in war we find worth,
But in love, compassion, and the power to give birth.

This Isn't What I Signed For

This isn't what I signed for, I never meant to be here,
I joined the Armed Forces, for what I thought was a career.
But fate had other plans, and duty called my name,
To the distant Falkland Islands, there flames of conflict came.

At eighteen, I stood proud, with naivety in my eyes,
Anxious heart beating fast, underneath vast South Atlantic skies.
The fog of war descended, over the ocean's endless blue,
A tempest of uncertainty, in a land I never knew.

The winds howled with bitter anger, as the waves crashed upon the shore,
The ground beneath my boots, echoed with the battles of yore.
In the trenches, side by side, brothers stood in arms,
We faced the brutal reality and were tested by war's harms.

But in the midst of chaos, in the face of fear and strife,
I witnessed bravery unyielding, and the resilience of human life.
We fought for home and country, for the principles we held dear,
We stood tall, we fought strong, with every ounce of courage clear.

Through the smoke and gunfire, I saw the strength of unity,
The bonds that formed forever, In the crucible of adversity.
Amidst the broken dreams, and the toll that war exacts,
I learned the measure of sacrifice, and the weight of comrades' pacts.

This wasn't what I signed for, but I found purpose in the fight,
To protect and serve with honour, in the darkest hours of night.
And when the battle's over, and the wounds begin to heal,
I'll remember what I fought for, and the camaraderie I feel.

For though this path was unforeseen, and the scars may never fade,
I found a family of warriors, in the Falklands' distant shade.
So let me stand as testament, io the young souls who wander,
That sometimes life's course alters and leads us where we ponder.

This wasn't what I signed for,
But it shaped who I became,
A soldier, forever marked,
By the Falklands' fiery flame.

Black Buck Mission

In the realm of distant Falkland's shores,
Where seas clashed and fierce winds' roars,
A tale unfolded, bold and grand,
Of Black Buck's mission, across the land.

Amidst the conflict's tumultuous might,
The Royal Air Force took to the flight,
Avro Vulcans, mighty wings in the sky,
To strike the enemy, swift and high.

With ascension from a distant isle,
They embarked on a daring trial,
Braving the vast and treacherous sea,
To reclaim what was meant to be free.

Through twilight's cloak, they stealthily flew,
In the cover of darkness, their path they drew,
Silent warriors, shadows of the night,
Guided by purpose, fuelled by the fight.

Over hostile lands, they ventured deep,
Their mission, secrets, they had to keep,
Slicing through the darkness, fierce and true,
To challenge the oppressor, the Argentine few.

Adversity and danger lay in their way,
But resolve and courage would never sway,
Evading the radars, enemy's gaze,
They pressed onward, undeterred in their blaze.

Cloaked by the land, they skilfully weaved,
Through valleys and mountains, undaunted, relieved,
Against a backdrop of rugged terrain,
They approached the target, a runway to maim.

In the midnight hour, the Vulcans appeared,
Like avenging spirits, their mission revered,
Low they descended, their engines' roar,
Striking fear in the heart of the enemy's core.

Bombs unleashed with thunderous might,
Pounding the land, shattering the night,
Explosions blossomed in a fiery dance,
A symbol of liberation, a daring chance.

Through a storm of fire, they fought their way,
As Argentine defences sought to sway,
Yet undeterred, they held their course,
For freedom's sake, with unwavering force.

Black Buck's warriors, heroes of the fight,
Their wings shining through the darkest night,
They struck a blow, a symbol of hope,
For a nation determined to reclaim its scope.

So let us remember, their unwritten tale,
Those unsung heroes, who fought without fail.
In the annals of history, their legacy shall dwell,
Honouring their sacrifice, with no 5-star hotel.

A Price To Pay

In the shadows of Mount Longdon, I lie,
A British soldier, with fading breaths and sighs,
The fiery battles waged, now a distant cry,
As the cruel hand of fate bids me goodbye.

Oh, how the cold winds of war did blow,
Upon this rugged land, so desolate and low,
With comrades by my side, we marched to and fro,
But now, I face the solemn dance with woe.

A bullet pierced my flesh, a searing pain,
As crimson rivers flowed, my life did drain,
In this forsaken moment, I shall not complain,
For it is the price we pay, our fate ordained.

I feel the weight of sorrow, heavy on my chest,
As memories of loved ones linger, unexpressed,
Regrets and dreams now mingle, unrepressed,
In this final hour, I yearn for solace and rest.

Oh, dear Mother, forgive your wayward son,
For leaving you behind, this battle won,
In death's embrace, my spirit shall be undone,
Yet my love for you, forever, shall brightly run.

To my sweetheart, so far away,
Know that in your absence, I long to stay,
But fate has decreed another path today,
Where love and life collide in disarray.

To my brothers in arms, fighting side by side,
In this sacred struggle, with honour we bide,
Though my spirit fades, my heart swells with pride,
For our sacrifice, in history, shall eternally reside.

As darkness descends, and the stars align,
I find solace in the heavens, so divine,
A soldier's journey ends, a soul to intertwine,
With the tapestry of courage, throughout time.

So lay me to rest, beneath this hallowed ground,
Where freedom's flame forever shall resound,
In the annals of history, my name may be found,
A fallen soldier, in eternal peace, I am bound.

"Letter From Mum"

Upon Mount Longdon's craggy face, where history unfolds,
A soldier's memory etched in stone, in tales yet to be told,
Mark Dodsworth, a medic brave, in B Company he stood,
In the Falklands' war, his life was claimed, in that rugged neighbourhood.

A letter from a mother's heart, in grief and deep despair,
She poured her love into those words, her pain, her endless care,
Unopened still, it rests among the rocks, a testament to her loss,
A mother's love forever sealed, her precious son, the cost.

"Dear Mark," she wrote, her trembling hand, a tear-stained paper sheet,
"Though you're gone from sight, my love for you remains complete,
In that distant land, on foreign soil, where you rest forevermore,
Know that in my heart, my darling son, your memory I adore.

The winds may howl, the snow may fall, on that distant mount so high,
But here, amidst these craggy rocks, your spirit will not die,
For every whisper of the breeze, and every starry night,
I feel your presence, near and dear, forever shining bright.

I long for you to open the letter, to hear your voice once more,
But it remains a symbol of the love that still does pour,
Through the cracks and crevices, in this sacred, rocky space,
A tribute to the sacrifice you made, in that distant, fateful place.

Rest in peace, my cherished son, among the stars so grand,
In heaven's embrace, you now reside, on an everlasting strand,
And know that here upon this mount, your memory will forever hum,
In the unopened letter from a mother's heart, a love that will never succumb."

Amidst the craggy rocks of Mount Longdon, in that hallowed case,
The unopened letter from a mother's heart, a tribute to her grace,
A symbol of the love and loss, a poignant, solemn drum,
In the Falklands' winds, it silently speaks — the letter from Mum

Make Sure You Mark The Dead

In the shadowed fields of battle, beneath a desolate sky,
Where heroes fought and bled, and many a brave soul did die,
A whispered command, a solemn creed, "Make sure you mark the dead,"
So history remembers the fallen, where they rest their weary head.

Amidst the chaos and the strife, in a land so far from home,
A solemn vow to honour them, across the moor, the sea foam.
Their names may fade with passing years, their stories left unsaid,
But their sacrifice shall not be lost, "Make sure you mark the dead."

In trenches deep and muddy, on a distant, foreign shore,
Young men of nerve stood their ground, their spirits tried and sore.
In the face of gunfire's thunder and the cries of comrades led,
The final plea echoed through the ranks, "Make sure you mark the dead."

Their dreams, their hopes, their futures, on the altar of war laid,
And as they fell, in solemn truth, the debt of honour paid.
Their rifles standing marked their resting place, bowed heads, soft words are said,
A promise to those who perished here, "Make sure you mark the dead."

The windswept Falklands whisper tales of battles long gone by,
Where history's chapters are written in tears from the sky.
But we, the living, carry forth the legacy that they spread,
For in our hearts, their memory lives, those marked among the dead.

And on this field of courage, 'neath an ever-changing sky,
We honour those who gave it all, with reverence in our eye.
Their sacrifice, a shining light, in the darkness it shall spread,
For when we say, "We will remember," we've truly marked the dead.

Remnants Of War

> Upon Wireless Ridge, where silence reigns,
> Linger remnants of fierce and deadly pains,
> Sniper's dance played out on desolate ground,
> Bullet cases scattered, stories unbound.
>
> Whispers of conflict still cling to the air,
> Echoes of battles, a grim despair,
> Brass casings glinting, a metallic sea,
> Witnesses to a war that once used to be.
>
> Each casing a vessel, a vessel of death,
> Fired with intent to steal someone's breath,
> Cold steel transformed into instruments vile,
> In a merciless game where lives were on trial.
>
> They lie there discarded, tarnished and spent,
> Once part of a weapon, now empty and bent,
> Inert shells of power that tore through the air,
> Leaving scars on the land, wounds too deep to repair.
>
> They tell of a time when darkness prevailed,
> When humanity's essence was cruelly curtailed,
> Soldiers as pawns, victims of might,
> On Wireless Ridge's crest, they fought their last fight.
>
> The wind whispers secrets, the ridge still holds,
> Tales of sacrifice, and stories untold,
> Bullet cases now silent, but history cries,
> For those who were lost under Falklands' skies.

So let them lie there, a sombre display,
A reminder of horrors that won't fade away,
On Wireless Ridge's soil, they rest and decay,
As a tribute to those who fell on that day.

The Mountains They Whisper

In the shadowed lands of the Falklands' shore,
Where the cold winds wail and the albatross soar,
Lay mountains of legend, where battles did rage,
Echoes of warfare, history's page.

Mount Longdon stood tall, a sentinel grim,
Where the fires of conflict burned at its brim.
Soldiers ascended, their fates intertwined,
Seeking the summit, not knowing what they'd find.

Two Sisters, they stood, side by side in the fray,
Witness to bloodshed, night turning to day.
The cries of the fallen, the clash of the steel,
The weight of the sorrow, too heavy to feel.

Tumbledown's slopes, steep and treacherous ground,
Where heroes were forged, and valour was found.
The fog of the war, the screams in the night,
Yet hope shone through,in mornings light.

Harriet's peak, overlooking the sea,
A battleground fierce, where many weren't free.
The echoes of gunfire, the smoke in the air,
A testament to those who dared to care.

Wireless Ridge, where signals did cross,
A strategic point, a significant loss.
The Morse code of war, dots and dashes of pain,
Yet from these battles, strength we did gain.

In the Falklands' embrace, these mountains did stand,
Silent witnesses to a war-torn land.
Though time moves forward, and memories fade,
The legacy of these battles will never degrade.

For in every stone, and in every gust,
Lives the spirit of warriors, the brave and the just.
And the mountains, they whisper, tales of yore,
Of the Falklands War, and the heroes it bore.

Chapter 4

Those Gone Before Us

> 907 people died during the Falklands war, 258 British and 649 Argentinian.
>
> Since the war more lives have been lost, civilian and military as a direct consequence of the events that year.
>
> This book only has words for a few of those people, and future writings will include more.
>
> We will remember them.

Petty Officer Kevin Stuart Casey (Ben) 846 Squadron, HMS Hermes

In Casey Cove, where memories reside,
Amidst the Falklands' rugged pride,
A tale of sacrifice we find,
Of a brave soul, forever enshrined.
Kevin Stuart Casey, Ben by name,

A hero's heart, engulfed in fame,
His Sea King soared amidst the night,
For country's call, he took that flight.
But destiny, with cruel intent,

Led them to a watery descent,
In the unforgiving, icy sea,
Petty Officer, Ben, fate's decree.
On that fateful night, 'midst storm and dark,

His Sea King crashed, leaving a grieving mark,
Presumed drowned, but in our hearts he'll stay,
Forever missed, until we meet one day.
The pilot rescued, saved from harm,

By HMS Hermes, a guiding arm,
But Casey, missing, presumed drowned,
In sorrow's grip, the family bound.
In forty years' time, the Isles would stand,

The Falklands honoured, a sacred land,
The Place Names Project, a tribute grand,
To heroes lost, a legacy planned.
Kim, his sister, her heart does yearn,

In Casey Cove, where spirits return,
A flight to Pebble, an island's grace,
so reveals a heavenly place.
Amidst the rugged cliffs and sea's embrace,

A piece of heaven, a sacred space,
In Casey Cove, where waves do kiss,
A brother's spirit, never to dismiss.
So let this poem be a heartfelt cry,

For Kevin Stuart Casey, who took to the sky,
In Casey Cove, his memory glows,
A beacon of bravery, forever it shows

Lieutenant Nicholas Taylor, Royal Navy HMS Hermes

Nicholas Taylor, a pilot I knew
Flew Harriers down South, in 82
The love of his life, being in the air
It was as if he spent his whole time there

The 4th of May he was given a task
A 3 ship attack is what was asked
Fly out to the East, head to Goose Green
Bomb what you can, without being seen.

From HMS Hermes he left, took off from the ramp
As fast as a bullet, headed for Camp*
On his way, to do some good
As he, and the crew, knew he would

From up in the air he could see the airstrip
Ready to bomb but anti air let rip
His Harrier exploded with him in his seat
In bits his aircraft the ground did meet

He didn't survive, he now lays at rest
In the place where he fought doing what he did best
Thanks to his skills, a war was won
Now off you go flying Sir, towards the sun.

> * Camp is any outlying settlement outside of the town of Port Stanley

Peter Ronald Fitton, 45 Commando Royal Marines

In memory of Peter Ronald Fitton, a brave Royal Marine,
Whose courage and honour in the Falklands was seen.
From the rolling hills of Leicestershire's land,
To the distant shores of a far-off strand.

He trained as a Marine with unwavering might,
Serving in Northern Ireland, ready to fight.
Promoted to Corporal, he rose with his grace,
A true warrior's spirit in every single place.

When the Falklands were invaded, duty called,
All leave was cancelled, as the nation was enthralled.
With 45 Commando, they journeyed 'Down South,'
On the RFA Stromness, they sailed with no doubt.

On that fateful night, as the world watched the sky,
Pete was part of a patrol, prepared to defy.
But in the chaos of war, tragically they fell,
Mistaken for the enemy, a sad tale to tell.

In Arbroath's Western Cemetery, he found his rest,
Among comrades and heroes, he was truly blessed.
A plaque in St Denys Church, his memory does keep,
In the heart of Leicestershire, where his loved ones weep.

Linda, his beloved, and their son, Derek by her side,
In 2013, the Elizabeth Cross, a nation's pride.
Presented by The Queen's Representative so dear,
In Pangbourne's chapel, where memories were clear.

As we honoured the 40th Anniversary, we recalled with grace,
The legacy of Pete Fitton in that distant place.
Fitton Bay, a tribute to his courage so bold,
In the Falklands' embrace, his story is told.

Peter, your sacrifice and bravery, we'll never forget,
A hero in life and in memory, we are forever in your debt.
In the pages of history, your name shall forever shine,
A Royal Marine, a true patriot, a hero of our time.

Phillip Anthony Sweet, 1st Battalion Welsh Guards

In memory's embrace, we hold a name,
A hero's tale, enshrined in eternal flame.
Phillip Sweet, a son of courage true,
Whose sacrifice in Falklands' skies we rue.

Upon the canvas of the open sea,
A chapter etched in history's decree.
In '82, on a fateful June day,
Sir Galahad met destiny's harsh sway.

Argentinian planes, a deadly dance,
Unleashed destruction with merciless advance.
Yet midst the chaos, 'midst the fiery fray,
Lies Phillip Sweet, forever there to stay.

A lance corporal with a heart of gold,
In duty's call, his story was foretold.
A nation's grief, a family's tears,
A loss endured through passing years.

But memory blooms in fields of thought,
In plaques and hills where he is sought.
Cut into stone, his name resides,
A symbol of courage that never hides.

Sweet Hill now rises, a solemn sight,
A tribute grand, for a man of fight.
Atop its peak, he watches over lands,
A guardian spirit with caring hands.

In whispers of the wind and ocean's song,
In the hearts of those who carry on,
Phil's legacy will forever thrive,
A symbol of bravery that will never dive.

So let us remember, let us hold dear,
The memory of Phillip, ever near.
In history's tapestry, his name is wove,
A tribute in verse to the love we'll always know.

Corporal Mick Melia, 59 Independent Commando Squadron

In the land where bravery blooms,
Amidst the Falkland's rugged looms,
A tale of courage, honour, and might,
A hero emerged in the morning's light.

Corporal Mick Melia, valiant and bold,
In battles fierce, his story told,
59 Independent Commando Squadron's pride,
With each step he took, by his comrades' side.

Attached to HQ A Company, 2 Para strong,
He faced the challenge, the battle's song,
On Darwin Hill, where conflict arose,
He stood unwavering, facing his foes.

As dawn broke on that fateful day,
Small arms fire echoed in disarray,
A Company came under the enemy's stare,
But Mick's courage shone bright, beyond compare.

With heart of a lion and spirit so true,
He fought for his nation, for freedom anew,
Though fate may have claimed him in strife,
His legacy lives on, in the tapestry of life.

In forty years' time, a tribute anew,
Melia Creek emerges, a tribute so true,
A namesake honoured, forever to last,
A symbol of strength from the past.

As waves kiss the shores of Melia Creek's shore,
His memory lives on, forevermore,
In the hearts of a nation, he finds his place,
A hero of Falklands, in time and in space.

Brian (Budgie) Marsden HMS Invincible

In memory of Brian "Budgie" Marsden,
Whose journey took him far from home,
A tale of youth and courage unburdened,
In distant seas where he would roam.

Upon HMS Invincible he stood,
Aircraft Handler, young and bold,
As Falklands' skies turned dark with blood,
His diary's pages would unfold.

Through Total Exclusion's Zone he'd sail,
A realm of danger, courage born,
Letters from home, a cherished trail,
Amidst the chaos, a hope reborn.

San Carlos' landing, fateful day,
His heart weighed heavy, fears untold,
Yet fate proved kind, and in dismay,
His premonitions did not unfold.

With entries penned, both joy and woe,
Surrender's relief, celebration's cheer,
The islands back, their flag aglow,
The War was over, the end was near.

Yet destiny weaves its threads unseen,
Two days past victory, a cruel twist,
Atrocious seas, a crushing scene,
Brian's light extinguished, sorely missed.

In Marsden Cove, his memory rests,
A sheltered haven, nature's embrace,
Among Falkland's beauty, his spirit quests,
A fallen hero, time can't erase.

So let us remember Budgie's name,
A life cut short, a tale well told,
In verses woven, his legacy aflame,
In history's pages, forever bold.

Surgeon-Captain Richard Tadeusz (Doc) Jolly OBE Royal Navy

In the realm of war, where courage meets grace,
There stood a hero, in a treacherous place.
Captain Jolly, his name etched in history's flight,
An angel of mercy, a guardian of life's light.

Amidst the Falklands' fury, where battles were rife,
He carved a haven of healing, saving countless lives.
At San Carlos' shore, where British forces trod,
He forged a field hospital, 'neath the gaze of God.

A disused abattoir, a refuge for the wounded,
With cramped walls and tainted air, their spirits remained grounded.
No Red Cross adorned the roof, a silent plea,
To protect the sanctity of a medical refuge's decree.

Brigadier Thompson's wisdom weighed in the fray,
Shielding the innocent, where conflict held sway.
For Captain Jolly, a mission took hold,
To mend broken bodies, to uphold stories untold.

In a realm of dirt and grime, where danger did loom,
He tended to the brave, amid bombs and sonic boom.
Two unexploded threats, a constant haunting dread,
But he stood undeterred, a rock amid the shred.

Over 580 souls passed through his caring hands,
A testament to his skill, where hope eternally stands.
Each life entrusted to him, a sacred vow,
And from his care, only three would fate allow.

Yet his compassion transcended borders and divide,
For he reached out to the Argentines, seeking ties untied.
He shared a list of lives, saved on the battlefield's breath,
Prompting truth to unfold, dispelling shadows of death.

Over fifty Argentine souls, traced by hands of fate,
Gathered in Buenos Aires, where gratitude would resonate.
In a reception of honour, their wounds forever scarred,
Captain Jolly, the saviour, their lives forever marred.

Argentina's Order of May bestowed its grace,
Upon this noble hero, in an unexpected embrace.
With foreign decoration, he sought the Queen's accord,
To wear the emblem proudly, as a symbol restored.

Her Majesty's reply, a testament of acclaim,
Authorizing his wearing, a legacy to proclaim.
Not for his solitary self, but for the medics who gave,
Their all on that battleground, where countless lives they saved.

Captain Jolly, a beacon of compassion and care,
His deeds intertwining the emblems of warfare.
A bridge between nations, a rare distinction held,
For both Britain and Argentina, his story swelled.

In the annals of conflict, where darkness holds sway,
Captain Jolly's legacy will forever stay.
A hero in healing, an emblem of peace,
May his name be remembered, and his virtues never cease.

Rest now, noble Captain, in the realm beyond,
Where valour is eternal, and battles are abscond.
Your selfless soul now free, from war's relentless might,
May your spirit soar high, in everlasting light.

Richard John De Mansfield Absolon MM, The Parachute Regiment

In respect of a soldier bold and true,
Let these words now pay tribute to you,
Private Richard John de Mansfield Absolon,
Whose bravery on distant shores was known.

Amid the South Atlantic's tempestuous air,
You ventured forth with unwavering care,
A scout and sniper in the Parachute Regiment,
Embarking on a perilous, noble ascent.

In the shadowed nights of Mount Longdon's domain,
You and your comrade, a courageous twain,
Inch by inch, closer to the enemy's sight,
Gathering intelligence in the cover of night.

With skill and coolness, undeterred by fear,
You sought their positions, drawing near,
For a Battalion's night assault, you paved the way,
Risking all for victory on that fateful day.

Rehearsing the path, you led your platoon,
Undetected, your actions a prelude to the moon,
Unveiling routes and foes with intricate care,
Ensuring your comrades would be prepared.

Then came the night, the hour of attack,
Mount Longdon called, and you led the pack,
Surprising the enemy with swift resolve,
Claiming a foothold, a moment to absolve.

In the heat of battle, you fought with might,
A man of courage amidst the fight,
Probing ahead, seeking the hidden threat,
Your aim true, a sniper's duty you met.

A single shot silenced a sniper's gun,
Enabling the Company's advance to be won,
With dash and determination, you pressed on,
An example of bravery, though youth had yet shone.

But alas, tragedy struck with the dawn,
Mortar fire claimed a life once drawn,
In the service of duty, you met your fate,
Leaving behind memories that resonate.

Private Absolon, a name etched in history's scroll,
Your coolness and bravery forever extolled,
A son of Mrs Pearce, who now mourns,
Your memory cherished, an eternal flame that burns.

In your gallant sacrifice, we find solace and grace,
May your spirit find eternal resting place,
In the annals of bravery, your name shall remain,
Private Richard Absolon, a hero we proclaim.

Sergeant Ian John McKay VC, 3rd Battalion, The Parachute Regiment

In the silent darkness of the Falkland night,
Where battles raged with fierce and daunting might,
A hero emerged, Sergeant McKay his name,
With courage and strength, he rose to fame.

The Parachute Regiment, their mission clear,
To seize Mount Longdon, dispelling all fear,
With 4 Platoon, B Company in the lead,
They faced the enemy, driven by their creed.

As bullets flew and shells tore through the air,
McKay's platoon pressed on, facing despair,
The ridge ahead held machine guns ablaze,
Their deadly aim threatening lives in a haze.

Amidst the chaos, their advance was stalled,
The platoon commander, wounded and appalled,
Command fell to McKay, a burden to bear,
With resolute spirit, he stepped forth to dare.

He knew the strength of the enemy's might,
Their positions fortified, hidden from sight,
Undeterred by peril, he made his decision,
To charge the foe and carry out his mission.

With three brave comrades, he broke from the rock,
Facing the firestorm, the deadly gridlock,
Their charge was met by a hailstorm of lead,
Yet McKay pressed on, undeterred by dread.

Amidst the chaos, losses began to mount,
A corporal wounded, a private's life counted,
But McKay, undaunted, pushed forward alone,
Resolute and fearless, his purpose well-known.

He stormed the enemy, with grenades in hand,
Unleashing fury, fulfilling his command,
The beleaguered platoons found a moment's grace,
Their positions relieved by McKay's embrace.

At the moment of victory, a hero fell,
His body upon the bunker, a sombre knell,
Sergeant McKay, selfless, his sacrifice made,
His courage and leadership, an eternal accolade.

In Aldershot's hallowed Military Cemetery,
His final resting place, an honoured sanctuary,
We remember McKay, his memory unswayed,
A shining example, in history's parade.

So let us stand and pay tribute today,
To Sergeant McKay, who showed us the way,
His gallantry, an inspiration so grand,
A true hero, forever etched in the sand.

Corporal David (Chuck, Mad Dog, Jock) Hardman, 2nd Battalion, The Parachute Regiment

In the fields of Meikle Earnock, he was born,
A brave soul destined for battles torn.
David Hardman, the youngest of four,
In Hamilton, Scotland, his spirit did soar.

Enlisting in the Army at sweet sixteen,
A boy soldier, his journey would begin.
With the Parachute Regiment, he found his place,
Training hard, preparing for a valiant race.

In '82, the Falklands called his name,
Corporal Hardman, his section aflame.
Leading his comrades ashore with might,
To face the enemy in the dark of the night.

Goose Green and Darwin, battles entrenched,
Against fierce opposition, their courage drenched.
David stood strong, a shield for his brothers,
Defending them bravely, as they fought for one another.

In the ill-fated assault, his life was claimed,
Yet his memory lives on, forever untamed.
Mentioned in Despatches, for bravery renowned,
A hero at rest, in Wellhall Cemetery's ground.

Each year, we gather, with reverence and grace,
To honour his sacrifice, his noble embrace.
David Hardman, a name etched in our hearts,
A brave soldier's legacy, never to depart.

Stephen Hood, 2nd Battalion, The Parachute Regiment

> Stephen, a Falklands War hero (Stephen took his own life in 2013).
>
> Whilst 258 British people died during the war, always
>
> remember those who died afterwards because of the war,

Amidst the turmoil and the strife,
A hero lived, a warrior's life.
Stephen Hood, with courage strong,
Marched into battle, where he belonged.

In Goose Green's shadow, he stood tall,
A paratrooper, giving his all.
Through the fire and the rain of war,
He tended wounds, saving lives galore.

A medic's touch, a gentle hand,
He brought solace to a wounded land.
With every life he fought to save,
He found purpose amidst the grave.

But deep within his weary soul,
Lingered scars that took their toll.
Flashbacks haunting his every thought,
A battle within, battles fought.

The war that never truly dies,
Reflected in his troubled eyes.
The memories he couldn't shake,
A heavy burden, hard to break.

In the quiet depths of his despair,
He sought solace, yet it wasn't there.
His silent anguish, his hidden pain,
Only whispers echoed through his veins.

And as the tensions rose once more,
Between the nations, at the core,
Stephen's heart could not withstand,
The weight of war upon the land.

In his car, where darkness fell,
Carbon monoxide's deadly spell,
Took him from us, far too soon,
Underneath the waning moon.

His widow's plea, a heartfelt cry,
To politicians soaring high:
Cease the sabre-rattling, the strife,
Let veterans heal from wounds of life.

For Stephen Hood, a hero true,
We salute you, and bid adieu.
May your spirit find eternal peace,
As your memory in our hearts increase.

In the annals of history, your name shall remain,
A symbol of bravery, a soul untouched by stain.
Rest now, dear Stephen, in tranquillity's embrace,
Your sacrifice remembered, your memory we embrace.

Shui Kam Yeung RFA Sir Tristram

In the seas of fate, a sailor's heart did beat,
From Cheung Chan Island, where his story took its seat,
Shui Kam Yeung, a name forever engraved,
A hero of the Falklands, valiant and brave.

On board the Sir Tristram, he sailed with pride,
A civilian crewman, with duty as his guide,
In the face of danger, he stood strong and true,
As the war-torn skies unleashed their deadly hue.

The bombs rained down, their fury unrelenting,
Yet Shui Kam faced the storm, undaunted and unyielding,
With courage in his soul, he fought till the end,
A symbol of resilience, a true comrade and friend.

In Fitzroy Creek, where bravery was shown,
He gave his life, so far away from home,
His spirit now sails on, in the ocean's embrace,
A guardian of the waves, forever in grace.

Oh, Shui Kam Yeung, your sacrifice we hold dear,
In our hearts, your memory will always be near,
With every wave that crashes upon distant shores,
Your legacy lives on, forevermore.

Sik Chee Yu RFA Sir Tristram

In the heart of Hong Kong, he was born,
Sik Chee Yu, from Kowloon's shores he'd drawn,
A bosun of the seas, a seasoned hand,
With Royal Fleet Auxiliary, he'd stand.

Years of service, on Sir Galahad he sailed,
With pride and courage, his duties never paled,
But fate had other plans, a war to face,
In Falklands' waters, he'd find his place.

April brought the call, to distant isles,
RFA Sir Tristram set sail, with hopeful smiles,
But on that fateful day, the skies turned grim,
As Argentine planes descended, dark and dim.

Alongside Sir Galahad, she stood,
Two sisters bound, in brotherhood,
Bombs rained down, and fast they did fall,
The ship was damaged, caught in a deadly thrall.

Amidst the chaos and the fire's blaze,
Bosun Sik Chee Yu met his final days,
With sorrow in our hearts, we weep,
For a soul lost, forever in the deep.

Yet, in our memories, he shall reside,
A hero fallen, but never denied,
On Falklands' Memorials, his name engraved,
Amongst the brave, forever saved.

Marchwood's Falklands Memorial stands,
A tribute to those who met war's demands,
To the men of RFA, lost in '82,
Sik Chee Yu, we remember you.

In every wave that crashes to the shore,
In every breeze that whispers evermore,
Your spirit sails, forever free,
Bosun Sik Chee Yu, in memory.

Sergeant Robert Arthur Leeming, 45 Commando

In the South Atlantic's vast expanse, a hero's tale unfolds,
Of Robert Arthur Leeming, courageous, strong, and bold.
A member of 45 Commando, a Heavy Weapons pro,
In '80, he made Sergeant, his skills aglow.

In the year of sorrow, '82, tragedy's cruel hand,
Took members of Mortar Troop, a heart-wrenching demand.
They landed at Red Beach, the Falklands' distant shore,
To fight for freedom's cause, to endure the war.

With comrades by his side, they yomped the rugged land,
Through Teal Inlet and Douglas, a united, brave band.
Towards Mount Kent they pressed, towards their final stand,
Bob showed unwavering resolve, a leader firm and grand.

On that fateful June day, during a reconnaissance patrol,
Mistaken for the foe, they faced an ambush whole.
In the crossfire of battle, on Two Sisters' hallowed ground,
Bob, and two comrades fell, their souls unbound.

His resting place in San Carlos, where the ocean breeze does roam,
A horseshoe-shaped corral, a soldier's final home.
With a view of Ajax Bay, where they once set foot ashore,
A tribute to their valour, their memory to restore.

So let us honour Robert Leeming's name,
A warrior's heart ablaze, in the chronicles of fame.
In sacrifice, he stood tall, for freedom and the right,
A guardian of justice, forever shining bright.

Captain Brian Johns Brice C Biddick, SS Uganda

Amidst the winds that swept the sea,
A gallant captain once set free,
Bound for Falkland's distant shore,
On the SS Uganda he'd explore.

With valiant heart and steadfast will,
He sailed the waves, a mission to fulfil,
But fate's cruel hand, it intervened,
And altered the course that lay unseen.

A malady struck, an illness dire,
Upon those waters, it lit its fire,
Though Uganda's deck was strong and grand,
It couldn't shield from life's harsh hand.

In irony's grasp, he took his bed,
Where surgery's blade was deftly led,
Aboard the ship, 'neath skies so vast,
A battle fought, but not to last.

Instead of journeys 'Down South' so far,
He underwent a desperate spar,
With life itself, a duel intense,
A struggle fought with no defence.

Repatriation came, a flight on high,
The RAF's wings carried him nigh,
To Wroughton's hospital, a sombre place,
Where life's dim flicker found its trace.

In eighty-two, the May bells rang,
When Captain Brian's spirit sang,
To the heavens, he bid adieu,
Leaving cherished memories for the crew.

Jill, his beloved, by his side,
Their love and bond could not subside,
Together, they faced life's stormy sea,
And from their love, a son was free.

Simon, a testament to love so deep,
In his father's footsteps, memories to keep,
Captain Brian's legacy lives on,
In tales of courage, in the setting sun.

With each ship that sails afar,
A whisper echoes, like a guiding star,
Of a captain brave, with a heart so true,
Brian Biddick, we remember you.

Lieutenant Commander John Edward Eyton Jones, Royal Navy, 801 Squadron,

In the Southern seas, where skies were grey,
A brave pilot soared 'midst fog and spray,
Lt Cdr John Eyton Jones, E-J they'd say,
A hero's tale on that fateful day.

Upon the deck of Invincible, he stood,
With seasoned skills, a heart of good,
To the Falklands he ventured, a mission's call,
To protect the lands, to answer the call.

Beside him flew Lt Al Curtis, bold,
Together they'd face the stories untold,
To investigate the radar's glow,
Near the Sheffield, resting in woe.

Through rain and fog, they took to the sky,
In two Sea Harriers, bravely they'd fly,
Through low cloud's shroud, they pressed ahead,
Where mysteries lay, their fate was led.

Oh, how the weather's fury raged,
A tempest's dance, their path engaged,
Yet E-J's expertise, his guiding light,
Navigating the darkness, morn barely in sight.

But as the dawn broke, a solemn hue,
Neither pilot returned, the skies askew,
The sea held its secrets, and it chose to keep,
The gallant souls who ventured deep.

Lost at Sea, the record reads,
A void remains, where sorrow leads,
His widow and daughters left to grieve,
In hearts, his memory they'll never leave.

In 2022, the islands pay their respect,
With Eyton-Jones Cove, a name to reflect,
A sandy beach where waves caress,
His spirit's home, a place to bless.

Rest in peace, Lt Cdr John Eyton Jones,
Your bravery hailed in nature's thrones,
In the books of heroes, your story shall live,
A pilot's courage, forever to give.

Lieutenant Commander John Murray Sephton DSC Royal Navy, HMS Ardent

In the South Atlantic's distant waves,
Where history's battles were engraved,
Amidst the courage and the loss,
A hero's tale, we shall emboss.

Lieutenant Commander John Murray Sephton,
With bravery and honour, his path was set on,
On May 21st, '82, in fierce attack,
HMS Ardent faced the enemy's track.

In San Carlos Water, the ship stood strong,
Against the Argentine Air Force's throng,
Bombs rained down, the sky ablaze,
And hearts were heavy, in a desperate phase.

The Seacat missiles lost, the odds were grim,
But Sephton's spirit refused to dim,
With resolute resolve, he took command,
And rallied his Flight to make a final stand.

Small arms they grasped, amidst the roar,
Defenders of the ship they swore,
In the face of danger, they pressed on,
Their courage shining like the dawn.

Upon the Flight Deck, he stood tall,
Directed fire to thwart the fall,
An A4 Skyhawk, it bore its wrath,
Yet he held fast, he blocked its path.

With submachine gun, held upright,
He faced the foe with all his might,
The moment brief, the sacrifice grand,
A hero's act, upon that land.

The bombs came down, the sky turned black,
Their target true, their deadly track,
But Sephton's bravery, it did shine,
An inspiration, an unyielding sign.

In that perilous hour, lives were lost,
But his courage held back the cost,
A beacon to the Ship's Company,
His legacy, an eternal decree.

In Falkland's heart, a place was found,
Sephton Island, on hallowed ground,
To honour him, his name does gleam,
Beside Lake Hammond's tranquil stream.

Now, let us remember this gallant soul,
Whose courage and sacrifice made us whole,
A hero, a husband, a father dear,
In our hearts, his memory we revere.

Radio Officer Ronald Hoole, RFA, Atlantic Conveyor

In the world of radio waves, Ronald Hoole stood tall,
A skilled and dedicated officer, he answered the call.
Through airwaves and frequencies, he bridged the divide,
Connecting distant worlds, with messages as his guide.

His adeptness with equipment, a master of the trade,
He navigated the ether, where words and signals played.
In a world of static and crackling sounds,
Ronald's voice emerged, clear and profound.

He reached out across the vast unknown expanse,
Sending and receiving, as if in a cosmic dance.
His voice, a conduit of connection and grace,
Weaving stories and news, to any time and place.

But destiny's hand dealt a tragic blow,
In the Falklands War, where heroes would go.
On the Atlantic Conveyor, Ronald Hoole set sail,
Unaware of the danger that would prevail.

Amidst the storm of battle, amidst the strife,
The Atlantic Conveyor faced a perilous life.
A missile struck true, with destructive force,
And tragedy swept through its very course.

In that fateful moment, Ronald Hoole fell,
His voice silenced, no more tales to tell.
A hero lost, his presence deeply missed,
But his spirit, undying, in our hearts persists.

For in the world of radio waves, his legacy endures,
His dedication and courage forever ensures.
That his sacrifice won't be in vain,
Forever, his name will remain.

Chan Chi Shing, RFA, SS Atlantic Conveyor

Chan Chi Shing, a laundryman with care so pure,
In his hands, fabrics found solace sure.
In the depths of the ocean, he found his peace,
His spirit lingers, memories will not cease.

Yet fate's cruel twist, a war's fierce tide,
Took him from shores, where dreams would glide.
Amidst Falklands' conflict, tragedy struck,
The Atlantic Conveyor, his vessel, amok.

With bravery he served, on waves so wide,
A laundryman turned hero, forever tied.
In the line of duty, his life was lost,
A sacrifice made, at great human cost.

His legacy lives on, in hearts that know,
The tale of a laundryman, who dared to go.
To seek solace deep in the ocean's embrace,
Where peace is found amidst life's turbulent race.

Chan Chi Shing, a soul gentle and kind,
In memories cherished, he'll always find
A place in our hearts, a hero so true,
His spirit endures, forever anew.

In the depths of the ocean, where he now rests,
Amongst coral reefs, he's forever blessed.
His spirit lingers, embracing the sea,
A laundryman's legacy, eternally free.

Ng Por, RFA SS Atlantic Conveyor

Ng Por, a laundryman with a gentle touch,
Diligently tending to garments and such.
In the Falklands War, tragedy struck his way,
When the Atlantic Conveyor was hit that fateful day.

Amidst the chaos and the battles fought,
Ng Por's life was tragically cut short.
In the sea's embrace, he found his rest,
A soul departed, but truly blessed.

Though he may not have held a soldier's gun,
His contributions were vital, though often unsung.
His humble role in the conflict's fray,
Washing away stains of war each passing day.

May his memory endure, a tribute to his name,
A reminder of those who suffered, their lives forever changed.
In the annals of history, let it be known,
Ng Por, a laundryman, his spirit will be shown.

Mark Steven (Doddy) Dodsworth - 3 Battalion, The Parachute Regiment

In memory of Mark Dodsworth, a brave soul,
Whose story we now share, for hearts to console.
A man so young, at seventeen he enlisted,
Into 3 Para, his journey persisted.

Quiet and unassuming, a gentle giant they say,
Doddy, his nickname, along the way would stay.
In Caroline Bankhead, he found his true love,
A marriage so short, a blessing from above.

Called back to his battalion, a medic he trained,
As fate would have it, his destiny ordained.
On his 24th birthday, a fateful year in '82,
The Falklands invaded, his duty he knew.

Deployed to action, his skills put to test,
Mount Longdon awaited, his courage the best.
Tending to the wounded, amid chaos and strife,
Doddy gave his all, risking his own life.

In the Battle for Longdon, tragedy befell,
A shot pierced his heart, a hero's farewell.
Just days before war's end, his sacrifice made,
The price of freedom, a debt never to fade.

His battalion endured, the losses so deep,
Twenty-three comrades in eternal sleep.
Three Days in June, etched in history's scroll,
A testament of bravery, engraved on their soul.

And in the Falklands, on the coast of the East,
Dodsworth Beach, a tribute, a place of peace.
Where waves gently caress the sandy shore,
Mark's spirit resides, forevermore.

Mark Dodsworth, beloved, forever young,
In our hearts and memories, your legacy sung.
A life cut short, but your spirit lives on,
A hero, a husband, a gentle giant, now gone.

Paul Green, 1st Battalion, Welsh Guards

In a land of distant shores and rugged might,
Where brave souls ventured into the Falkland's fight,
There stood Guardsman Paul Green, so strong and true,
A hero with a spirit, steadfast and anew.

Born in St Asaph, a town of humble grace,
Paul's journey began, his destiny to embrace,
Joined by his brother, united in their aim,
To serve their nation, honour etched in their name.

As fate would have it, they were set apart,
To face the challenges, each with a valiant heart,
Paul sailed with Welsh Guards, the Sir Galahad his ship,
Unaware of the trials, ahead on his trip.

June 8, 1982, a day forever etched in pain,
When bombs rained upon them, in Fitzroy's domain,
The Sir Galahad suffered, tragedy unfurled,
And in that fateful moment, we lost our beloved world.

Amidst the grief and sorrow, his mother found solace rare,
A visit to Falklands, a bittersweet affair,
Standing by the San Carlos cemetery's hallowed ground,
A whisper in her heart, a calling she had found.

Her burdens lifted, a new chapter had begun,
Ann sought a refuge where healing could be won,
The Falkland Islands beckoned, with open arms it called,
A place where love and loss entwined, forever enthralled.

Forty years would pass, a tribute came alive,
To honour Paul's memory, his name will forever survive,
Green Bay, a testament to his bravery untold,
A name forever etched in stories yet to unfold.

So let us remember, the heroes brave and true,
Like Guardsman Paul Green, with skies of vivid blue,
In the annals of history, their stories shall remain,
Echoing through time, their memories we shall retain.

Seargent Ian Nicholas (Kiwi) Hunt, Special Boat Service

> The 2nd of June, a day to remember
> When blue on blue collided together
> Neither knew each other was there
> Because command chose info not to share
>
> But Ian Hunt, an SBS Sarge
> Lost his life that day, to an SAS charge
> His death was even extra dire
> As there is no such thing as "friendly fire"
>
> Nicknamed Kiwi, now of late
> Died so young, just 28
> His place name on East Falklands, should you seek
> Lies on the banks of Kiwi Creek.

Corporal Michael David (Doc) Love DSM, 846 Squadron

> In the dusk of time, our tale begins,
> A bond of friendship, now marked by pins.
> Forty years have passed, yet I still recall,
> The day we lost you, dear friend, our Doc Love.
>
> On that fateful flight, to distant shores,
> A Sea King soared, carrying hopes and more.
> Amidst the SAS troops, you stood so strong,
> A pillar of courage, forever gone.

The helicopter's blades sliced through the air,
Heavy with burden, but you were aware.
To lighten the load, fuel levels were reduced,
Unbeknownst to us, it was fate that seduced.

At three hundred feet, a descent underway,
A chilling thump echoed, stealing the day.
Another followed, a cry in the sky,
And then, dear Doc, the Sea King took its dive.

Within seconds, a plunge into the deep blue,
Life shattered, dreams scattered, and hearts subdued.
Some lives extinguished, others left stunned,
As the waves claimed our hopes, one by one.

Miraculously, a handful escaped the cold sea,
Nine brave souls who fought to be free.
But you, dear Doc, trapped within that craft,
Taken from us, leaving our hearts wracked.

Theories abound, of what caused the dread,
An albatross's flight path, overhead.
Did it collide, interrupting the course,
Taking you, dear friend, with such brute force?

The SAS mourned, their loss profound,
Eighteen soldiers gone, never to be found.
And I, your friend, left with memories dear,
Haunted by the day you disappeared.

Dear Doc, your spirit forever remains,
Etched in our hearts, eternal in our pains.
Your selfless service, a legacy untamed,
For which the Distinguished Service Medal was named.

Now, four decades have drifted away,
Yet your presence lingers, in every way.
In the stories we share, the laughter and tears,
You're with us still, dispelling our fears.

Today, I honour you, my dear departed friend,
With this heartfelt poem, a tribute to send.
Forty years may have passed since we said goodbye,
But your memory, Doc Love, will never die.

Jason Burt, Neil Grose and Ian Scrivens, 3rd Battalion, The Parachute Regiment

Upon the windswept heights they stand,
On Mount Longdon's storied land,
Three souls so young, their lives untamed,
In memory's embrace forever named.

Private Burt, at seventeen's dawn,
With courage fierce, his spirit drawn,
To serve with honour, heart held high,
Beneath Falklands' vast and open sky.

Grose, whose youth just reached eighteen,
Yet in his eyes, a fire keen,
He marched with purpose, bold and strong,
In the face of battle's wild song.

And Scrivens, aged seventeen still,
Answering duty's steadfast thrill,
His steps resounding on foreign soil,
A patriot's heart, a noble toil.

Sergeant Southall, firm and true,
With dedication pure and blue,
He placed a plaque upon that hill,
A testament to those young hearts' will.

In memory's embrace, they rest,
Their sacrifice, our hearts attest,
Forever bound by honour's chain,
On Mount Longdon, they shall remain.

So let us remember these souls so young,
Whose valorous deeds and songs unsung,
Their names etched deep in history's scroll,
In Falklands' tale, a noble role.

Colour Sergeant Gordon Findlay, David Parr and Francis Slough, 2nd Battalion, The Parachute Regiment

In the midst of the Falklands' battle cry,
Upon Wireless Ridge, 'neath the open sky,
Three souls of courage took their stand,
Fighting their fight, in a foreign land.

Gordon Findlay, a Colour Sergeant true,
Led his comrades with a steadfast view,
His voice so strong in the chaos and din,
Guiding his men through the strife within.

Private David Parr, a brave soul so young,
His spirit unwavering, his song unsung,
He fought with a fire, a fierce burning light,
For freedom's cause, through day and night.

And Private Francis Slough, gallant and strong,
Among the warriors who stood, headlong,
In unity and sacrifice, they stood as one,
Facing adversity until the battle was done.

Upon Wireless Ridge, their steps did trace,
Writing their names in history's embrace,
In their Regiments name, they gave their all,
Answering the battle's fervent call.

Their sacrifice, a poignant tale,
Of heroism where courage set sail,
In memory's keep, they shall forever reside,
As stars that guide us through the night sky wide.

On the 13th and 14th of June's embrace,
In Falklands' fields, their spirits grace,
Gordon, David, and Francis, in eternal rest,
Among the bravest, they are truly blessed.

Let us remember these souls so bright,
Whose valorous hearts still shine with light,
On Wireless Ridge, they found their place,
In history's pages, their courage we embrace.

Chapter 5

Respite – The Wildlife

> The archipelago is known for its abundant wildlife, both on land and in the surrounding waters. The variety of bird species, marine life, and mammals make the Falkland Islands a unique and important habitat.
>
> Albatrosses, known for their impressive wingspans. Penguins, including king, gentoo, rockhopper, magellanic, and macaroni species.
>
> Marine mammals, such as sea lions, elephant seals, and fur seals inhabit the coasts and surrounding waters. The Falkland Islands are a prime location for observing whales and dolphins, with at least fifteen species in the area. There are numerous species of birds, including birds of prey like the striated caracara.

The Big Brown Seal

In the Falkland's rugged land so wild,
Where nature's beauty is undefiled,
A big brown seal finds its reprieve,
Upon the rocks, by the restless sea.

With fur as rich as the earth's deep hue,
It scratches itself with a joyful clue,
In the golden sun's warm embrace,
This creature finds its tranquil space.

Its whiskers glisten with ocean's kiss,
As waves dance 'round, in eternal bliss,
In this remote and pristine domain,
Where wildlife thrives, free from disdain.

On rocky shores, where the wild winds sweep,
The seal finds solace in slumber's keep,
A sentinel of nature's grand design,
In the Falkland's embrace, divine.

With each scratch, it sings a song,
Of ancient rhythms that belong,
To this untamed, rugged coast,
Where nature's beauty is foremost.

So let us cherish this pristine sight,
In the Falkland Islands' purest light,
For in this seal, scratching free,
We glimpse a world of wild beauty.
In daylight's gentle, golden hue,

Black Crowned Night Heron

In daylight's gentle, golden hue,
Upon an old shipwreck, weathered and true,
Stands a black crested night heron, so serene,
A solitary sentinel, a majestic scene.

Its plumage dark as the midnight sky,
With a crest that touches clouds up high,
It perches on the beam, ancient and worn,
A sentinel of time, a treasure reborn.

The ship, once proud, now rests in decay,
But the heron stands firm, come what may,
Its ebony feathers, a stark contrast to wood,
A sentinel of nature, misunderstood.

With keen eyes, it scans the waters below,
In search of fish, its movements slow,
Graceful as the ship's ghostly memories,
It embodies the past, as the ocean breeze carries.

Amidst the wreckage, a story unfolds,
Of adventures and journeys, untold,
And the heron, a witness to history's grip,
A symbol of resilience, on this weathered ship.

So, let us admire this feathered king,
With a black crested crown, it takes wing,
On the beam of the shipwreck, it stands tall,
A reminder that beauty thrives amidst life's fall.

The Seaweed Blanket

On a sandy shore, where the elements embrace,
Lies an elephant seal in tranquil grace,
Wrapped in seaweed, like a blanket of the sea,
A creature of majesty, wild and free.

Beneath the sun's golden, shimmering light,
In the quietude of day, and the peace of night,
The seal finds solace on this sandy bed,
Where dreams of ocean depths dance in its head.

Its massive form, a testament to might,
Yet in repose, a gentle, peaceful sight,
With eyes that hold the wisdom of the tides,
In this haven, where tranquil beauty resides.

The seaweed, like a tapestry, does drape,
Across the seal, in nature's quiet cape,
A gift from Neptune's kingdom, pure and green,
A cozy shroud, a refuge, serene.

Each strand, a memory of the deep blue sea,
Where life beneath the waves, in harmony,
With kelp forests swaying, and secrets untold,
The seal, in its seaweed, finds stories unfold.

As stars above twinkle in the night's embrace,
The seal slumbers on, in this tranquil space,
A sentinel of nature, a guardian of the shore,
Wrapped in seaweed's embrace, forevermore.

So, let us cherish this moment in time,
When nature's wonders in harmony chime,
An elephant seal, in its seaweed sheet,
A symbol of beauty, in restful retreat.

The Penguins

In the Falklands' land, where battles were fought,
Where the bullets flew and the tension was taut,
Amidst the chaos and strife, a sight to behold,
Were the penguins waddling, brave and bold.

With feathers all fluffy, and bellies round,
They wandered the beaches, unbothered by sound.
Bullets whizzed by, but they didn't care,
As they strutted and squawked, without a single scare.

Their little black suits, all dapper and neat,
Made them look like secret agents, oh so discreet.
They'd gather in groups, huddling tight,
Plotting their penguin revolution in the moonlight.

While soldiers patrolled and tanks roared past,
The penguins had a party, they had a blast!
They slid on their bellies, like sleek little spies,
Unaware of the danger that loomed in the skies.

And as the bombs exploded, the penguins danced,
They did the tango and the penguin prance.
They flapped their wings and honked with delight,
While battles raged on throughout the night.

The soldiers would pause and gaze in awe,
At these funny creatures, without a flaw.
For amidst the chaos, they found solace and peace,
In the penguins' resilience and their carefree release.

So, here's to the penguins, heroes so true,
Who carried on, no matter what they'd been through.
They remind us to find joy, even when times are tough,
And that laughter and love are more than enough.

In the Falklands' tale, where bullets flew by,
The penguins united under the open sky.
They showed us the power of mirth and play,
In a war-torn land, where they waddled away.

The Humans Came

In the realm of the wild, where the penguins play,
And the albatross soars at the break of day,
A tale unfolds, of a time of dread,
When the sky turned dark, and the earth bled.

We, the creatures of land and air,
Watched in silence, in despair.
The thunder of guns, the flash of light,
Shattered the peace of the night.

The humans came, with fire and steel,
In our home, they made their deal.
The hills echoed, with cries of war,
In the land where silence was, before.

We watched from afar, from our rocky shore,
As they fought and fell, and rose once more.
Our home, our haven, a battleground,
Where the echoes of conflict, still resound.

Yet, we endured, in our silent way,
Through the darkest night, to the brightest day.
The war ended, the humans left,
In our home, of peace bereft.

Now, we roam, in our land once more,
On the windswept plains, by the ocean's roar.
The echoes of war, a distant cry,
Under the endless, Falkland sky.

We, the creatures, the silent witness,
To a time of sorrow, a time of distress.
In the realm of the wild, where the penguins play,
We remember the war, in our own way.

Feeling Sheepish

In a land where sheep roamed, oh so fine,
A battle unfolded, a tale quite divine.
The Falklands War, 'twas a clash so absurd,
With woolly warriors that you've never heard.

Argentina stood tall, all mighty and grand,
But the sheep had a plan to take back their land.
They bleated in unison, "We'll take the fight!
For our meadows, our pastures, we'll unite!"

With fleece as armour, they charged through the fields,
Their hooves pounding thunder, breaking all shields.
The Argentinian army, they quivered in fright,
As the sheep stampeded with all their might.

With a baa here and a baa there,
The sheep had no need for human warfare.
They outsmarted the foes with cunning and grace,
With tactical grazing, they won the race.

The Argentinian soldiers were puzzled and lost,
As sheep planned their moves with precision, no cost.
They nibbled on documents, ate battle plans,
Leaving the enemy army in desperate hands.

With sheepish grins and woolly pride,
They triumphed over Argentina, far and wide.
The Falklands were saved, their victory sweet,
The sheep had proved they were quite elite.

So remember this tale when you're counting sheep,
They're more than just fluffy, they're tough and deep.
For in wars bizarre, where unlikely paths tread,
Even sheep can emerge as heroes, it's said!

Chapter 6

Mothers, Fathers, Brothers, Sisters, Wives, Girlfriends.

> When your loved one goes off to war each day is a worry,
>
> Sometimes, they don't come home. Sometimes, when they do they are so changed mentally that they are not the person who went.
>
> The time in war for all involved can lead to a lifetime of trying to cope with what happened.

Is It Worth The Fight?

In shadows cast by war's cruel hand,
A family waits on shifting sands,
For the husband, once their guiding light,
Returning from fighting, a shattered knight.

He once wore a uniform, proud and tall,
Now bearing the scars of a brutal thrall,
His eyes, once bright with hope and love,
Now haunted by the stars above.

A spectre of the man he used to be,
Haunted by memories, never set free,
He walks through rooms with a vacant stare,
A stranger now, in his own lair.

The children, once so full of glee,
Now hush their laughter, fear to see,
The darkness in their father's eyes,
As he fights the demons that never die.

The wife, who longed for his embrace,
Now hides her tears, her heart's disgrace,
She tends his wounds, both seen and deep,
While her own soul slowly falls asleep.

In the quiet hours of the night,
She wonders if it's worth the fight,
To hold onto a love now marred,
By the war that left their lives scarred.

For war, it takes and never gives,
Leaving behind shattered lives it sieves,
And though the battles may be won,
The war's true toll is never done.

In the silence of their home's abyss,
They grapple with the pain, the miss,
Of a family torn, a life unmade,
By the darkness war has cruelly laid.

So, let us not forget the cost,
Of battles fought, of lives now lost,
For in the quiet of the night,
The shadows of war cast their blight.

Imagine

I imagine the fear, I imagine the pain,
The things that you went through, are stuck in my brain
The job you loved doing, the job you did well,
Created my nightmare, and makes my life hell.

The news of you down there, in the papers we saw
The letters you had written, then the knock on the door.
I imagine the fear, I imagine the pain
I can feel your lungs bursting, from the air as it drained.

Your ship slowly sinking, there was no way out,
Stuck in your workplace, no-one to shout.
I know you were thinking, of me as you went,
To the bottom of the ocean, then heaven sent.

I imagine the fear,
I imagine the pain.
Those thoughts always haunt me,
And drive me insane.

meeting the parents

In the depths of restless slumber, shadows creep,
An unyielding torment haunts your mind's keep.
As the gentle waves whisper a solemn refrain,
Memories of war ignite the flames of pain.

Upon the deck, amidst the chaos and dread,
A sailor's duty embraced with steadfast tread.
Bodies engulfed in an inferno's cruel dance,
Your hands bore witness to life's fleeting chance.

The acrid stench of burning flesh still lingers,
Echoing the cries of anguish, ghostly fingers.
Within your heart, a searing brand of remorse,
For lives lost in battle's unforgiving course.

Their faces, once vibrant, now etched in your soul,
Their stories untold, swallowed by war's dark toll.
Men who stood beside you, brothers through strife,
Now mere whispers, fading remnants of life.

Through tortured dreams, their spectres arise,
Their pleas for solace pierce through weary skies.
Their eyes, beseeching, haunt your waking hours,
Their pain entwined with a sailor's fragile powers.

And in England's embrace, the voyage complete,
You find yourself standing, trembling, heart's beat.
The weight of their absence, an agonizing weight,
As you face their parents, their hearts laid bare, innate.

In trembling steps, you approach their waiting kin,
Words falter on your lips, lost amidst the din.
The grieving eyes that search for solace in your own,
A mirror to the wounds that your spirit has sown.

Their tears cascade like rivers, merging with the sea,
A shared sorrow, a testament to lives set free.
You offer solace in silence, a tender embrace,
A sailor's compassion, a salve for grief's grace.

For in the crucible of war's relentless strife,
You carried their burdens, stitched the threads of life.
Though scars remain etched deep within your core,
Your presence, a testament, forevermore.

So sail on, weary sailor, through memories and pain,
Know that your spirit, in darkness, shall remain.
For in your torment lies an undying light,
A testament to courage, in war's endless night.

A Mothers Anguish

In the midst of joyful hearts, I stand alone,
Amongst wives, girlfriends, and parents, as one.
A sea of celebration engulfs the air,
Yet my soul is consumed by despair.

HMS Hermes returns with pride held high,
Bringing back heroes, their battles fought nigh.
But my beloved son, Nick Taylor, my light,
Was taken away, lost in the Falklands' fight.

I see tears of relief, hear laughter and cheers,
Embraces of loved ones, erasing their fears.
Yet my arms ache for the touch of my own,
For the son I nurtured, now forever gone.

How can I find solace in this bitter scene,
When all I see is what might have been?
My heart clings to memories, etched deep within,
A bond unbreakable, where love had once been.

Each passing day, a reminder of my loss,
An endless void, an ocean I must cross.
I yearn to hear his voice, to see his smile,
To hold him close, if only for a while.

But fate has dealt a cruel and heavy blow,
And now I'm left with sorrow's bitter flow.
Grief wraps around me like an iron shroud,
As I mourn the son buried 'neath the shroud.

Yet amidst the darkness, a glimmer of light,
In the memories cherished, I find respite.
Though he may not be present by my side,
His spirit, undying, forever will abide.

So, I stand here in the midst of their cheer,
With tears in my eyes, masking the fear.
I honour the heroes who made it back home,
But in my heart, my son, you'll never roam.

For in this gathering of joy and pain,
I find solace in knowing you're not in vain.
Your courage, your sacrifice, forever enshrined,
In the annals of history, your legacy defined.

Though I may never hold you in embrace,
I'll forever cherish your memory's grace.
In the depths of my despair, I'll still hold on,
To the love that transcends, even when you're gone.

So, amidst the celebration, I stand tall,
A mother's love, unyielding through it all.
In the homecoming of Hermes' crew,
I find solace, dear Nick, for I remember you.

My Dad

In the airport, I stand so small,
Waiting for my dad, brave and tall.
He went to fight in a distant land,
The Falklands War, where heroes stand.

Soldiers in line, uniforms the same,
I join them too, in my own little frame.
Clutching my mum's hand, filled with fear,
As the plane descends, drawing near.

My heart beats fast, excitement and dread,
Hoping to see my dad, alive, not dead.
But as the doors open, my hopes take a fall,
For there is no smile, no voice to call.

Instead, a coffin appears before my sight,
The colours so solemn, wrapped in white.
Tears well up, my young heart aches,
Reality crashing down, no more mistakes.

I wanted to see him, hug him tight,
Tell him I missed him, day and night.
But now he's gone, forever it seems,
Lost in a war, the cruellest of dreams.

My little hands shake, my voice can't speak,
As tears stream down, wetting my cheek.
The weight of grief, so heavy to bear,
A child's world shattered, it's just not fair.

Oh, Dad, I miss you, in every way,
I wish you could have come home to stay.
But I'll remember your courage, your love so deep,
In my heart, forever, your memory I'll keep.

As I stand here, a young soldier so small,
In my dad's honour, I'll stand tall.
Though my innocence fades, I'll find strength anew,
For my hero dad, I'll make him proud, it's true.

In Shadows Deep

In shadows deep, where sorrow dwells,
A mother's heart, a tale it tells.
With tear-stained eyes and heavy sighs,
I grieve the loss, my spirit cries.

In tender youth, a boy so fair,
With dreams untold, he took the dare.
A soldier bold, his heart aflame,
To distant shores, his fate became.

The Falklands called, a battlefield,
Where valiant souls would never yield.
He marched away, my brave young son,
To face the horrors that war had spun.

Amidst the chaos, death's cruel embrace,
A mother's love, no shield in place.
In dreams I held him, safe and sound,
But reality struck with grief profound.

Oh, cruel fate, you dealt your blow,
My precious child, why did you go?
A mother's love, now torn apart,
Forever etched upon my heart.

The pain so raw, it knows no end,
A void inside, no words can mend.
I hear his laughter, feel his touch,
Yet only memories bring him such.

The empty crib, the silent room,
A life extinguished, too soon, too soon.
His laughter echoes in the breeze,
But now it's naught but memories.

The world moves on, time marches by,
But grief remains, it does not lie.
A mother's love, forever weeps,
For in my heart, my sorrow seeps.

Oh, sweet child, forever missed,
Your absence leaves my soul abyssed.
In dreams I'll hold you, close and tight,
Until we reunite in eternal light.

So here I stand, a broken vessel,
A young mother's pain, no words can wrestle.
But in my sorrow, I find some solace,
That love endures, beyond life's malice.

For in my heart, forever enshrined,
A bond unbroken, pure and kind.
And though you're gone, my precious one,
Your spirit shines, a brilliant sun.

So I will weep, but also strive,
To keep your memory alive.
Through tears and pain, I'll carry on,
In your honour, my brave young son.

The Poems

It's very hard to sit here,
Reading all these poems,
The pain that's shooting through me,
Only God in heaven knows.

Each word, a bittersweet reminder,
Of a son taken too soon,
His laughter, his dreams, his future,
Now etched on battlefields strewn.

These verses paint a picture,
Of a war fought across the sea,
But in my heart, it's personal,
For my son, the casualty.

The rhythm of these lines,
Echoes the very beat of my heart,
A symphony of sorrow,
A melody torn apart.

They speak of courage, they speak of loss,
Of comradeship, of sacrifice,
But my tears fall, unspoken,
For a life I can't entice.

Every muscle aching with longing,
For just an embrace, one more day,
Oh, how I yearn for that chance,
For my dear son to stay.

The verses may bring solace,
For others in this dark abyss,
But for me, they unveil wounds anew,
An unrelenting, painful twist.

Yet, I'll read them all, despite the ache,
For within those lines, I find,
A glimpse of my son's spirit,
A piece of his soul left behind.

In every word, he lingers,
A testament to love and pride,
So, I'll gather strength, read on,
With him forever by my side.

For as these poems tell their tales,
Of heroes lost in that distant fight,
I'll hold my son's memory close,
And find solace in the words, so bright.

Though it's hard to sit here, I'll endure,
For in these poems, he lives on,
And through the pain and sorrow,
My love for him will never be gone.

Why Did They Go?

Why did they go to the Falklands, why did they go to war?
In the depths of sorrow, my heart forever torn.
A brother lost in battle, a life that was so dear,
His spirit now adrift, in oceans crystal-clear.

With heavy hearts we ponder, the choices made back then,
Could peace have been the answer, without these losses grim?
A quest for resolution, through politics and talks,
To find a common ground, on peaceful, hopeful walks.

The islands, vast and distant, a land both wild and pure,
Became a stage for conflict, where pain would now endure.
The drums of war were beating, the nations locked in strife,
And in the crimson shadows, we bid farewell to life.

Yet, in this sea of sadness, a question lingers on,
Could peace have been the answer, where lives were never gone?
The hindsight of tomorrow, a lesson we must glean,
To guide us in the choices, that shape the future's dream.

But let us not forget, the bravery and the might,
Of those who gave their everything, in that relentless fight.
They answered duty's calling, stood firm on foreign shores,
With courage and conviction, against the lion's roar.

For they believed in justice, in freedom, and their land,
Their sacrifice a testament, to values strong and grand.
And though we mourn their absence, our souls forever scarred,
Their memory shall endure, like a sentinel standing guard.

So, let us seek the solace, that words of peace can bring,
To heal the wounds of battle, and let forgiveness sing.
May nations find a pathway, to harmony's embrace,
Where dialogue and understanding can bring conflicts to a trace.

Why did they go to the Falklands, why did they go to war?
A question that still echoes, deep within our core.
But in the midst of darkness, let love and hope arise,
To build a world united, where peace can harmonise.

News Of My Son

In the quietude of my humble abode,
A mother's heart sits heavy, bearing a massive load.
Through the windowpane, I gaze, longing for a sign,
An emblem of hope, a glimpse of divine.

My son, a brave soul, in the Falklands he fights,
A sailor of ships, adrift on distant nights.
In the Royal Navy he sails, with courage and might,
Anchored by duty, his spirit shining bright.

Each passing day, my worries they grow,
Tossed by the tempest, in this ebb and flow.
Whispers of battles and tales of strife,
Engulf my soul, like a blade searing life.

The clock ticks slowly, hours fade away,
My heart, it trembles, fears start to sway.
With every breath, anticipation takes hold,
For news of my son, a story yet untold.

Then, as the sun's golden rays kissed the land,
A knock at the door, like a siren, did command.
My trembling hands, they reach for the handle,
A moment of truth, I can scarcely handle.

A stranger stands before me, eyes full of pain,
His voice a mere whisper, as if in refrain.
Words, like daggers, pierce my fragile heart,
Shattering dreams, tearing worlds apart.

"Madam," he begins, his voice breaking,
"Your son, a hero, his spirit forsaking.
In the line of duty, he fought till the end,
A son, a comrade, a brother, a friend."

Silence descends, a shroud of despair,
My heartache unfolds, a burden to bear.
I cradle my grief, in the depths of my soul,
Tears, like rivers, cascade, they take their toll.

A life extinguished, a flame dimmed too soon,
Bound by the ties of a nation in tune.
Yet, in my anguish, I find solace, profound,
For he walks with heroes, on hallowed ground.

In memories cherished, I hold him near,
My heart full of love, forever sincere.
His memory enshrined, in the tapestry of time,
A son of the ocean, a spirit sublime.

So, I sit here, a mother, forever changed,
With a heart that's scarred, yet never estranged.
For my son, my sailor, though he may be gone,
His legacy, forever, in my soul will live on.

How I Wept

I was 18 when we sailed to the Falkland Islands on HMS Hermes, had my 19th birthday down there. My brother also served down there on HMS Antelope. when I left my mother was young, when I came back she had grey hair. although my brothers ship was sunk he survived. here is a poem written in the eyes of my mother)

In the stillness of my humble abode,
A mother's heart, burdened with heavy load.
Two sons, my pride, sailing far away,
To Falklands' shores, where battles held sway.

In the Royal Navy, their duty called,
Their spirits bold, their resolve enthralled.
With each passing day, anxiety grew,
Praying fervently, their safety I pursue.

Then came the news, a chilling refrain,
One ship struck down, engulfed in pain.
My heart sank deep, my spirit crushed,
A tempest of fear, my soul thrashed and rushed.

Days turned to nights, and nights into days,
My mind ensnared in a tangled maze.
I clung to hope, a flickering flame,
Searching for solace, a whispered name.

Oh, how I wept, tears carving my face,
In the shadows, seeking solace and grace.
The sea, my companion, relentless and vast,
Bearing witness to prayers that I cast.

And then, like a candle, a glimmer of light,
A whispered rumour, dispelling the night.
My child, my flesh, had cheated death's hand,
Saved from the depths by a miracle's strand.

A flood of relief, a torrential release,
Joy intermingled with lingering grief.
For one was saved, while others were lost,
A bittersweet victory, a heavy cost.

Now reunited, my children, so dear,
Embracing the love that banishes fear.
The scars of battle etched deep in their souls,
Yet resilience and courage continue to unfold.

For all those mothers, bound by a similar thread,
Whose sons and daughters bravely fought and bled,
May hope be your compass, your strength, and guide,
In the darkest hours, love's torch abide.

And though the echoes of war may still ring,
May peace find its place, and healing springs.
For my sons, forever bonded by the sea,
Their survival, a testament to resilience and me.

How do I tell them

How do I tell them he's not coming home,
To face the anguish, the sorrow unknown?
A young wife's heart, now shattered and torn,
In the wake of a battle, where hope was forlorn.

The Falklands War, a distant battleground,
Where Countries clashed and heroes were found,
But amidst the glory and victories claimed,
Lies a painful truth that cannot be tamed.

I hear their whispers, their worried queries,
Asking for news, hope in their eyes, so weary.
The children, innocent, unaware of the storm,
Yearning for a father, their hearts so warm.

But how do I tell them, their hero has fallen,
That fate has dealt us a blow so solemn.
That dreams once shared will never unfold,
In a tale of loss that will forever be told.

I clutch his letters, stained with love's embrace,
Seeking solace in words he left in his trace.
His voice echoes through the lines on the page,
A love eternal, transcending life's cage.

In tears, I pen my sorrow and despair,
The weight of grief, too heavy to bear.
But I find strength in memories we hold dear,
In the laughter, the love, in each passing year.

So I gather my courage, I wipe away tears,
For our love, though tested, will conquer our fears.
I'll tell them gently, with a heart full of grace,
That their father's spirit forever we embrace.

We'll honour his sacrifice, his strength and might,
And teach them to cherish the stars in the night.
For though he's gone, his love will remain,
In every heartbeat, in each tender refrain.

How do I tell them he's not coming home?
With courage and love, so they're not alone.
We'll face tomorrow, hand in hand, as one,
And in his absence, a family, forever strong.

Always A Tomorrow

There is always a tomorrow,
despite the thoughts going around your head.
Memories of those who fought with you,
the heroes who lay there dead.

In your eyes, I see the weight you bear,
the burdens of war, the scars you wear.
But know, my love, you're not alone in this fight,
Together we'll conquer the darkest of nights.

I long to see that spark in your eyes,
To hear your laughter that echoes the skies.
I yearn for the warmth of your tender embrace,
To see the lines of worry slowly erase.

The echoes of battle may linger on,
But I'll hold your hand till the pain is gone.
With every sunrise, a chance to renew,
To heal the wounds and make dreams come true.

For you are not defined by the battles you've fought,
But by the love within you, the lessons they taught.
Embrace the memories, honour the fallen with pride,
But remember, my love, you're still by my side.

There is always a tomorrow, my dear,
Where hope can triumph over every fear.
Together, we'll find solace in love's tender embrace,
And bring back the smile upon your face.

In the depths of your heart, a hero resides,
A warrior who faced turmoil with strength as his guide.
But let me remind you, my love, of your worth,
Beyond the battlefield, a life filled with mirth.

So let the haunting memories slowly fade,
As we embark on a journey, a new escapade.
I'll be here, steadfast, through the highs and the lows,
As love's gentle current continuously flows.

There is always a tomorrow, my love, never forget,
That together we'll conquer the demons we've met.
For in each other's arms, we'll find solace and peace,
And restore the joy that makes our love increase.

So take my hand, my brave and resilient knight,
Let us rewrite your story, bathed in love's light.
Together we'll build a future, strong and true,
Where the battles of yesterday won't define you.

There is always a tomorrow, my heart whispers in delight,
A future where your spirit can soar to new heights.
And as we navigate life, hand in hand, side by side,
You'll find the peace you seek, my love, within our love's stride.

Broken Fragments

> I'm sorry I couldn't handle it, war changed you oh so much,
> The battles that consumed your mind, the scars that softly touched.
> We walked a path so treacherous, the aftermath severe,
> And though my heart, it bled for you, I couldn't quell my fear.
>
> You were the man I cherished, the one I held so close,
> But war's relentless grip, my love, had stolen you the most.
> Your eyes once filled with laughter, now haunted by the past,
> The weight of countless burdens, a sorrow meant to last.
>
> I saw you in your darkness, your soul adrift at sea,
> Searching for the fallen, you couldn't come back to me.
> Their faces etched upon your heart, their voices in your dreams,
> A battlefield that lingered, tearing at the very seams.
>
> I tried to be your solace, to heal your wounded soul,
> But war had left its mark, my love, and took away control.
> You turned to distant shadows, lost in memories deep,
> And as I reached out for you, you slipped away, my keep.
>
> The man I married long ago, so full of light and grace,
> Was slowly fading, drifting into a far-off place.
> I longed to see your smile again, to hold you through the night,
> But war had left you hollow, a candle losing light.

So I made the painful choice, to let our love release,
To find some semblance of the man who found his peace.
I mourned the loss of what we had, the dreams that slipped away,
But love, I had to set you free, to find your own sunray.

I hope one day you'll find the peace, the solace that you seek,
To mend the broken fragments and hear your spirit speak.
For though we've gone our separate ways, my love for you remains,
And in my heart, the memories of love's bittersweet refrains.

I'm sorry I couldn't handle it, war changed you oh so much,
But in my heart, you'll always be the one I'll always clutch.
I wish you strength and healing, on this journey that you tread,
And hope someday you find the peace that war has left unsaid.

The Bond

In shadows cast by sorrow's hand, our hearts entwined, a broken band,
A tale of love, once strong and true, now rent apart, by loss and rue.
In distant lands, where courage soared, our son, a hero, he bravely poured,
His soul, his dreams, his youthful might, for freedom's call, he took his flight.

But fate, unkind, with cruel embrace, snatched him from us, his tender grace,
A sacrifice we cannot bear, a wound that leaves us both laid bare.
Our home, once filled with laughter's gleam, now echoes of a shattered dream,
In silent corners, grief holds sway, tears stain the memories of our yesterday.

We tried to stay, to face the ache, but sorrow's weight, too much to take,
Our souls adrift, in separate pain, in solitude, we seek to find refrain.
Divided paths, we now must tread, with broken hearts and spirits dead,
Yet, in this verse, I reach to you, to heal the wounds, to find some solace too.

For though we're torn, our love remains, a bond unbroken, through life's strains,
In cherished moments, side by side, our son's sweet spirit shall ever reside.
Let's think of him, with love profound, by lifting ourselves from grief's dark shroud,
Embrace the memories, tender and dear, and find the strength to persevere.

For in the depths of sorrow's grasp, our souls entwined, in this painful clasp,
Let's forge a path, with love's embrace, rebuilding lives, with gentle grace.
May time's gentle balm bring us release, and bring a whisper of lasting peace,
Though apart, may our hearts still mend, together, in love, until the end.

In this poem, my ex-husband dear,
I reach across, through loss and tears,
To share a bond that nothing can sever,
For you and I, we'll endure forever.

Innocence Lost

In shadows cast by love's once gentle embrace,
Lies a tale of sorrow and a haunting trace.
Once upon a time, our hearts danced in accord,
But the tempest of war left wounds to be explored.

A union woven in affection's tender thread,
With dreams of bliss and a future widespread.
But fate's cruel hand played a treacherous role,
As distant shores beckoned with a thunderous toll.

The Falklands' call summoned my love away,
To serve with honour, in skies tinged grey.
A sailor he became, a hero in strife,
But little did we know the cost of his life.

Beneath the distant stars, battles raged fierce,
And a spirit once gentle faced horrors severe.
Upon his return, I held him with hope,
But the man who returned wore a different cloak.

His eyes, once bright, held shadows profound,
Haunted by echoes of a battleground.
War's cruel embrace had stolen his grace,
And etched upon his soul, pain's hardened face.

Innocence lost, he was a wounded soul,
An empty vessel, love could not console.
The nightmares that haunted him in sleep's abyss,
In the waking hours, became an unbearable twist.

His anger, once foreign, now fueled his rage,
A storm unleashed upon this sombre stage.
I, the target, bore the brunt of his pain,
As love's serenade transformed into disdain.

But still, I remember the love we once shared,
The dreams and hopes that once beautifully flared.
With every scar and every tear that falls,
I pray for healing, as love eternally calls.

For deep within his shattered heart, I believe,
A glimmer remains, a chance to retrieve
The love that once bloomed in gardens untamed,
And cast away the darkness that has claimed.

In this prison of anguish, we find solace sought,
Hoping our love's fire can never be bought.
For love's true power can conquer despair,
If only we find the strength to repair.

So, I'll endure the tempest and carry the weight,
Seeking the dawn, though the hour is late.
In love's resilient arms, we may yet find release,
From the shackles of torment, finding inner peace.

For love, like a phoenix, can rise from the flame,
And in its embrace, heal all wounds that came.
Together we'll forge a path to reclaim,
The love we cherished, the love that remains.

It's Been Many Years Passed

In the quiet of the night, when the world's at rest,
I hear the whispers of the south wind's jest.
It carries tales of a land so far,
Where my love met his fate, beneath a foreign star.

The Falklands, they said, a place so cold,
Where stories of valour and bravery are told.
But to me, it's a land of sorrow and woe,
Where I lost my love, many years ago.

His letters spoke of battles, of courage and might,
Of comrades and kin, who'd fight the good fight.
But between the lines, I felt his fear,
The uncertainty of war, drawing ever near.

The day the news came, the world turned grey,
My heart shattered, my dreams swept away,
He was gone, taken by the sea's cruel hand,
Lost to the waves, in a distant land.

It's been many years passed, but the pain's still raw,
The wound in my heart, an ever-present flaw.
I see him in dreams, hear his voice in the breeze,
Feel his touch in the shadows, his warmth in the trees.

The world moved on, but I remain still,
Haunted by memories, against my will.
For in the Falklands, where the cold winds blow,
Lies a part of my heart, buried deep in the snow.

Chapter 7

War Children

> *I have had the pleasure of speaking with some of the children of those we left behind.*
>
> *They were so young at the time that it is difficult for them to remember what their dads were like but mum has made sure they grew up knowing the heroism shown by dad.*
>
> *It is part of our duty as veterans to ensure these boys and girls, now men and women, know that they are a part of us, as their dads used to be.*

Were you thinking of me?

Were you thinking of me, Dad, as I think of you,
In a land far away, where the sky was once blue?
Did thoughts of your little boy cross your brave mind,
As you fought for others, leaving no love behind?

You were a hero, Dad, with a heart so pure,
Defending the innocent, valiant and sure.
With each step you took on that distant shore,
You embodied courage, a icon to adore.

In my dreams, I see you, tall and strong,
A protector, a guide, even when things went wrong.
You taught me kindness, and to always be brave,
But now I'm left wondering, how do I behave?

Mom says you're watching from the heavens above,
But why did you leave us, with tears and no love?
The pain in my heart feels too heavy to bear,
I miss your warm smile and the touch of your care.

Were you thinking of me, Dad, as you faced the fight?
Did memories of my laughter bring you light?
I wish I could hear your voice, hold your hand tight,
To tell you, "I love you," with all of my might.

Though you're gone, your spirit forever will stay,
In the stories we tell, and the games that we play.
I'll grow up, remembering the hero you were,
And cherish the moments, however few they were.

So, here's to you, Dad, my brave guiding star,
I'll carry your memory, no matter how far.
In my heart, you'll live on, forever true,
And I'll keep thinking of you, as I miss you too.

Eyes Open

In a world of innocence, a tender heart does dwell,
A child with untold stories, a tale no words can tell.
But a storm has come upon this soul, an unexpected blow,
For the teacher seeks the father, who fought so long ago.

In the land of Falklands, where battles waged with might,
A hero stood with honour, defending what was right.
His spirit soared so high, amidst the ocean's roar,
But fate had other plans, and his life did deplore.

Now the child stands before the class, emotions running deep,
A yearning for his father, a pain he cannot keep.
The teacher, unaware of the wounds that lie inside,
Speaks of absent fathers, igniting tears the child can't hide.

Oh, how does one explain the grief that words can't heal,
To a child whose father's touch, he's never again to feel?
The teacher seeks connection, but stumbles unaware,
That her demand for presence brings anguish to bear.

In a corner of the classroom, the child softly weeps,
Searching for a way to cope with secrets that he keeps.
But within his fragile heart, a strength begins to rise,
A flicker of resilience, a fire in his eyes.

He takes a breath, his voice determined, though it quivers yet,
"Teacher, my father is a hero, in my heart he's set.
He fought a noble battle, in a land so far away,
But he won't return to me, no matter what you say."

The room falls into silence, as truth hangs in the air,
The teacher's eyes now open, understanding growing there.
She steps towards the child, with empathy so clear,
Wrapping her arms around him, banishing his fear.

"Forgive me, little one, for my lack of empathy,
Your father's love is boundless, a timeless legacy.
I'll honour his memory, and hold your heart so dear,
Together we'll navigate a path devoid of fear."

The child, embraced by kindness, finds solace in her touch,
A bridge of understanding, where pain and sorrow clutch.
And in that moment's grace, a healing love begins to mend,
A teacher and her student, their bond will never end.

For though the child's father rests in a distant foreign land,
His spirit lives forever, as a guiding, gentle hand.
And in the halls of learning, where wisdom's seeds are sown,
A tale of love and loss, through poetry, is known.

A Child's Loss

Why don't you have a daddy, the other children shout,
Their words like arrows piercing my heart, filling me with doubt.
At six years old, the weight of loss is very hard to bear,
The absence of a father's love, an emptiness so unfair.

I see their smiles, their laughter with their dads,
While I navigate this world with a void that makes me sad.
Why did fate choose this path for me, so steep and grey?
In the midst of innocence, I learned sorrow's price to pay.

The Falklands took my father, a hero, brave and true,
Defending distant lands, he bid this world adieu.
Memories I hold are but fragments of a dream,
A father's loving touch, his voice, forever unseen.

I long to hear his laughter, to feel his warm embrace,
To see him wipe my tears away and kiss my tiny face.
But destiny had other plans, tearing us apart,
Leaving behind a little child with an aching, wounded heart.

I wear a smile upon my face, to hide the tears I've shed,
To mask the pain that lingers on, trapped within my head.
But in the stillness of the night, when darkness starts to fall,
I yearn for his presence, to hear his voice once more, his call.

Oh, Daddy, why'd you have to leave me all alone?
In a world that feels so cold, where my heart has turned to stone.
The other children have no clue, the pain they put me through,
For they still have their daddies, while I'm left without a clue.

So as the years go by, and I grow older day by day,
I'll cherish the memories I have, though they're too far away.
And maybe, just maybe, in some distant realm above,
I'll find my daddy waiting there, to fill my life with love.

So, children, please remember, before you tease and shout,
That not everyone's journey is filled with laughter, without a doubt.
For some of us, the world is a little darker, a little grey,
So be kind and understanding, for you never know what others hold at bay.

My Darling Child

In the cradle of life, you lie serene,
A tiny soul, yet to be seen.
Unaware of the world's sorrow and strife,
My precious one, soon to taste life.

But, my child, before you draw your first breath,
I must impart a tale of grief, of death.
Your father, a sailor, so brave and strong,
In the Falklands War, where he belonged.

Upon the restless sea, he sailed away,
To protect our shores, night and day.
A hero's heart, he carried with pride,
His love for us, an unwavering guide.

Amidst the waves and raging fight,
He stood valiantly, against the night.
But fate can be cruel, as we sadly know,
A battlefield's price, it took him below.

A sea of tears, my darling, I've cried,
For the man I loved, the father denied.
In dreams, he walks with us once more,
But waking brings sorrow, grief at the core.

Yet, my unborn child, you must understand,
Your father's courage, like grains of sand,
Shall live on in you, forever true,
A legacy of love he passed on to you.

Though he rests beneath the ocean blue,
His spirit remains, forever in you.
With every breath you take and smile you share,
I'll see his reflection, know he's still there.

As you grow, my love, and start to explore,
The world's vast ocean, the distant shore,
Remember your father's love was grand,
His sacrifice, a bond that'll forever stand.

Though this tale is filled with sorrow's art,
May it forge strength in your tender heart.
For even amidst the darkest night,
Love's enduring fight will guide you to the light.

Your Chair is Still There

In a quiet room, where memories reside,
A chair sits empty, by the fireside.
It's been years, but the pain's still raw,
For the son whose father, went to war.

The tales of valour, of courage so grand,
Of soldiers who fought, on that distant land.
But for this young boy, just one tale remains,
Of a ship that was sunk, and the heartache it gains.

The laughter they shared, the games they would play,
All seem like dreams, now far, far away.
The medals and honours, to the brave they bestow,
But what of the void, that only he knows?

He's grown over the years, tall and so fair,
Yet he looks to the chair, and wishes him there.
The world moved on, as it always will do,
But in that silent room, time stands still, it's true.

The stories of war, of heroes so great,
Are told and retold, as matters of state.
But for the boy, now a man, with tears in his stare,
The war's only story is, "Your chair is still there."

Chapter 8

After The War

> The anguish is over. There is never a winner in war, only losers.
>
> The Islanders have spent the rest of their lives being grateful to those who came in the name of freedom. Most of those that went band together, tell stories, comfort each other, whilst some sit in silence - remembering.

Class of 82

In the pages of history, a tale unfolds,
The Class of '82, their stories told,
Not students, but veterans of war's cruel test,
Soldiers, Sailors, Airmen, the bravest, the best.

From distant lands they came with resolute hearts,
Answering duty's call, playing their parts,
No textbooks, no lectures, just battles to face,
In the Falklands, they stood with unwavering grace.

Heroes they became, each one, every role,
With courage unyielding, they claimed their goal,
Through the tempest of conflict, they sailed and they soared,
Their dedication and sacrifice forever stored.

Soldiers on the frontlines, fierce and strong,
Marching 'midst chaos, where right and wrong,
Merged in the fog of the battlefield's haze,
They held their ground through nights and days.

Sailors who navigated the unforgiving sea,
Guiding ships with purpose, bound and free,
Their unity and prowess, the waves could not sway,
As they forged ahead, come what may.

Airmen who soared in skies of uncertainty,
Their wings carried hope in the face of adversity,
Guiding the flight of freedom with every stride,
In the vast expanse, they wouldn't hide.

Civilians who stepped forth, undaunted, bold,
Side by side with the uniformed fold,
From medics to engineers, each played their part,
Stitched wounds and built bridges with a steadfast heart.

In unity they stood, a tapestry diverse,
A symphony of courage, each note a verse,
Though roles differed greatly, their spirits aligned,
For freedom, for justice, they all combined.

So let us remember the Class of '82,
Not students, but heroes, whose valour we view,
Soldiers, Sailors, Airmen, and the brave civilian band,
Their legacy lives on, united they stand.

In the journals of time, their stories persist,
An eternal flame of courage, in each heart's mist,
They knew the risks and took them, no retreat,
The Class of '82, in our gratitude, we greet.

Liberation Day

In the land where waves crash upon the shore,
Where freedom's spirit forever soars,
There lies an island, brave and bold,
Where tales of valour and courage are told.

On Liberation Day, a joyous decree,
The Falkland Islands stood proud and free,
With spirits unyielding, hearts filled with might,
They reclaimed their home, bathed in liberation's light.

Amidst the Atlantic's tempestuous embrace,
A battle was fought, leaving its trace,
The islanders united, their resilience aflame,
In the face of adversity, they carved their name.

Marching through the fog, a daunting quest,
For freedom's call, they never rest,
With valour and honour, they faced the storm,
Their love for the land forever warm.

From San Carlos to Stanley, their footsteps tread,
The echoes of their courage, forever spread,
With each wave crashing against the shore,
The spirit of liberation forevermore.

Oh, Falkland Islands, a place of might,
Your journey to freedom shines so bright,
On this hallowed day, we honour your fight,
And celebrate your triumph in radiant light.

May your flag fly high, in winds so strong,
For the men who came to right the wrong,
Liberation Day, a timeless tale,
Of a land unyielding, where heroes prevail.

So let us raise a toast, in unity we stand,
To the Falkland Islands, a liberated land,
May your spirit endure, forever bold,
A testament to the power of freedom untold.

I Don't Know You

    I don't know you but I know you were good.
    I don't know you but I wish that I could.
    I don't know you but I know that you died.
    I don't know you but I know your mum cried.

    I don't know your name, but I feel your spirit,
    In the stories they tell, your courage, I hear it.
    You fought in a war so far from my home,
    In the Falklands, where the wild winds did roam.

    You stood for a cause, with honour and pride,
    In a battle for freedom, you bravely did stride.
    Though I never met you, your sacrifice clear,
    In my heart, I hold you, a hero so dear.

    Your comrades remember the battles you fought,
    Through the darkest of times, the lessons you taught.
    They speak of your laughter, your unwavering grace,
    In the harshest of moments, in that faraway place.

    Though we never crossed paths, our lives so apart,
    I hold you close now, deep within my heart.
    For you are the reason I can live without fear,
    In the land that you fought for, your memory is near.

    To the man I never knew, but I wish that I had,
    Your bravery and valour, they make me feel glad.
    Though time has passed on since that fateful day,
    In my thoughts and my prayers, your spirit will stay.

So here's to you, soldier, though we never did meet,
In this poem, your memory, forever complete.
I don't know you, but I'll always be grateful you stood,
For the freedom we cherish, in a place understood.

A Job To Do

Soldiers are strong, The enemy weak,
Adventure and fame, Is what you should seek.
A long row of medals, high on your chest,
Be proud of your kills, now go get the rest.

And whilst you are out, on the hunt for your pray,
The men that command you, in the office all day.
Sitting and planning, lighting the fuse,
Looking all smart, in their shiny shoes.

The enemy must die, send in the boys,
Supply them the kit, but not all the toys.
We want heroes to praise, it makes us look good,
All medals are shining, in rows heroes stood.

And after, in meetings, we've no money to fund,
Nice shiny equipment, or high-powered guns.
Politicians not caring, they don't give a toss,
Our men not returning, an acceptable loss.

And once leaving the army, they are on their own,
No funding, no training, to the streets they are thrown.
But whilst you're a hero, of that it's true,
Go out kill the enemy, you've a job to do.

Liberty Lodge

Liberty Lodge, a place of peace for those who fought and shed their tears, whose memories still haunt their dreams, whose scars still burn like open seams.

Here they can come to rest their minds, to walk the hills and breathe the air, to see the sea and feel the wind, to find some peace from all their care.

Here they can meet with friends and family, to share their stories and their pain, to laugh and cry and talk of life, and find some comfort to keep them sane.

Liberty Lodge, a place of hope, for those who still bear the scars, who still remember the war, but know that they are not alone.

Here they can come to heal their hearts, to find some solace and start anew, to know that they are not forgotten, that their sacrifice is not in vain.

The Rules In My Head

In the depths of our souls, questions arise,
As we ponder on life's twists and its ties.
Why do we reminisce with fondness and grace,
On moments that caused our hearts to embrace?

Unpleasant experiences, though they may be,
Hold lessons and growth for us to see.
Our minds, wondrous machines, filter the past,
Extracting the good, discarding the vast.

Through years of existence, we've carried along,
Ideas and teachings that seemed so strong.
But why couldn't we fit in this foreign domain,
Amidst emotions, resentment, and disdain?

The world, once so narrow, confined in its space,
Appeared one-dimensional, devoid of embrace.
Yet within our own rules, a sanctuary we found,
Shared only by those we left on that ground.

Where are the comrades, the ones by our side,
Who covered our back, whatever betide?
Separating past and present, a daunting task,
While honouring those we lost, wearing a mask.

So many questions, it's answers we seek,
As memories and stories intertwine and speak.
Moving forward, the quest of our soul,
For years, it perplexed, took its heavy toll.

But behold, the solution, clear as the morn,
A loving home, a good woman, not torn.
Two kids, full of light, with talents that bloom,
And grandkids, blessings, with futures to groom.

Amidst it all, a new set of rules we decree,
To guide us forward, our spirits set free.
For in love and in family, we find our release,
A testament to life's newfound peace.

So let the questions subside, let them rest,
In the warmth of our hearts, we have been blessed.
With gratitude, we move forward, hand in hand,
With our self-imposed rules, a purpose so grand.

What Could Have Been

This is about a young soldier killed in the Falklands War, the poem is about what could have been.

In the land of the living, an untold tale,
A love unbroken, that would never fail,
A young soldier's path diverged from despair,
To a future of hope, a love beyond compare.

In the Falklands' shadow, where battles cease,
A life of peace emerges, a tender release,
He meets a lady fair, a soul so bright,
Whose love illuminates the darkest night.

Their hearts intertwine, two souls become one,
A union blessed under the radiant sun,
In tender moments, their love would bloom,
A symphony of laughter, dispelling all gloom.

Together they'd walk, hand in hand,
Exploring the world, a united band,
Through meadows and mountains, they'd travel afar,
Writing a story more brilliant than any star.

And within this narrative, a spirit anew,
A child of their love, their dreams coming true,
With eyes like oceans, reflecting their grace,
The embodiment of their eternal embrace.

Guided by love's compass, nurtured with care,
A bond unbreakable, a future so rare,
They'd teach lessons of kindness, compassion's worth,
Igniting a flame of empathy from birth.

In this alternative tapestry of life,
Each moment a treasure, free from strife,
The soldier turned father, a pillar so strong,
Protecting his family, righting every wrong.

Together they'd celebrate life's every phase,
In laughter, in tears, through joyous displays,
With every passing year, their love would deepen,
A testament to the life they're all steeped in.

Though this reality lies in the realm of dreams,
Where fantasy thrives and hope forever gleams,
Let it be a reminder of love's precious grace,
To cherish every moment, in any time or place.

For within our spirits, the past and the now,
We hold the power to create and allow,
A legacy of love that transcends time's tether,
In the world we build, in the bonds we treasure.

Faithful Companion

In the realm of loyalty, a bond untold,
A tale of love, of courage, to unfold.
Amidst the battles, where chaos would reign,
A faithful companion, through heartache and pain.

Oh, noble dog, with eyes so bright,
You sensed my absence, day and night.
As I embarked upon a distant shore,
You waited patiently, forevermore.

Through lonely days and starlit nights,
Your paws on the doorstep, eager for sights.
You couldn't fathom why I had to go,
Leaving behind the walks we used to know.

But deep within your soul, you understood,
A sailors duty, the call for good.
And when I returned, weary and scarred,
You wagged your tail, my truest guard.

Beside me, steadfast, you stood so strong,
A pillar of solace when things went wrong.
Through battle's nightmares and troubled dreams,
You soothed my spirit, mended the seams.

With every step, you walked by my side,
A friend and confidant, in whom I confide.
Your presence, a balm for my troubled mind,
A bond unbreakable, a love so kind.

In the Falklands' echoes, where memories reside,
You shared my burdens, my fears you defied.
With unwavering devotion, you taught me anew,
The power of companionship, steadfast and true.

So, here's to you, my faithful friend,
A love that time can never transcend.
In the depths of my heart, you forever dwell,
A beautiful dog, my saviour, I can tell.

Standing Tall

In the depths of battle's cruel embrace,
I stood upon Falkland's sacred space.
Where friends were lost, their spirits set free,
Their memory etched in eternity.

The haunting echoes of gunfire past,
Forever etched in my soul so vast.
Their faces, now mere shadows in my mind,
I search for solace, longing to find.

But bitter shall I not forever be,
For their sacrifice, I must truly see.
In every sunrise and every breeze,
They whisper gently, calming my unease.

I choose to honour, to carry their light,
To live my life, and sleep at night.
No mood swings shall cast a darkened spell,
I'll rise above, their story to tell.

For in this journey, I find my strength,
To live with purpose, no matter the length.
To honour the fallen, their dreams and fears,
To cherish their memories throughout the years.

In each passing moment, I'll wear their pride,
With every step forward, they'll walk beside.
For they didn't return, but I'm here to stay,
To live with respect, come what may.

So let the bitter winds of sorrow fade,
As I embrace life, not burdened by shade.
I'll stand tall, for them, with every breath,
Their legacy cherished, even in death.

And when my time comes, as it surely will,
I'll join them once more, my heart calm and still.
For in their presence, I'll find eternal peace,
Their souls embraced, never to cease.

So, fellow traveller, let us together be,
A testament to those who couldn't see,
The light beyond conflict, the love that remains,
In our hearts, forever, their memory sustains.

Remnants Of War

In the hush of dawn, when the guns are still,
And the smoke of battle has had its fill,
The Falklands stand, in eerie calm,
A landscape scarred, yet bearing balm.

The echoes fade, the soldiers gone,
Only remnants of war, to look upon.
Helmets hollow, boots bereft,
Silent stories, of those who left.

The trenches dug, now graves for none,
Mark the path of a war hard won.
Barbed wire fences, rusted, torn,
Speak of a time, when peace was shorn.

Yet, in this silence, life stirs anew,
In the golden gorse, in the morning dew.
The penguins return, to their rocky shore,
The albatross soars, as before.

The hills remember, the sea keeps score,
Of the war that came to this distant shore.
Yet, they stand resilient, in the southern sea,
The Falklands, a testament to tranquillity.

In the eerie calm, memories haunt,
Of the brave, the fallen, the dauntless jaunt.
Yet, in the whispers of the wind, one can find,
A land healing, leaving war behind.

For in the aftermath, in the quiet dread,
Life persists, and hope isn't dead.
In the eerie calm, after the battle's roar,
The Falklands breathe, forevermore.

Let the Tears Flow

In the heart of the valley, where the rivers do wind,
Lies a tale of a war, of the most brutal kind.
The waters once clear, now tainted with red,
Echoes of battles, where many have bled.

The river, it flows, with a sorrowful sigh,
Carrying memories of those who did die.
Its currents are heavy, with the weight of the lost,
The price of a war, an immeasurable cost.

Mountains weep silently, their shadows cast low,
For the souls that were taken, let the tears flow.
The ripples tell stories of heroes so brave,
Yet now they lie silent, in a watery grave.

The trees on the banks, once green and so tall,
Now stand as mourners, witnessing the fall.
Their leaves fall like tears, on the river's sad course,
A reminder of war's unrelenting force.

The wind carries whispers, of the pain and the woe,
Of families torn apart, with nowhere to go.
The river, it weeps, for the lives that were stowed,
In the depths of its belly, let the tears flow.

For war is a monster, that consumes all in sight,
Turning day into darkness, and love into spite.
But the river, it promises, as it continues to go,
That even in darkness, hope can still grow.

So let the tears flow, like the river so deep,
For the memories of war, we forever will keep.
And as the waters cleanse, may we come to know,
The price of our actions, let the tears flow.

Oh Falklands Winds

Amid the Falklands' cold embrace they lie,
Beneath the pale moon's mournful sigh,
A land once untouched by war's cruel hand,
Now holds the fallen, a desolate band.

The bitter winds sweep o'er lifeless forms,
Where once was laughter, now silence storms,
Unyielding frost on faces so young,
Their stories unfinished, their songs unsung.

In fields where hope and dreams did bloom,
Now broken hearts and sorrow loom,
A canvas of pain painted in grey,
As cold winds steal their warmth away.

No more do they hear the lark's sweet song,
No more do they rise with the dawn's first throng,
Gone are the days of laughter and mirth,
Replaced by the cold embrace of the earth.

Oh, Falklands' winds, how cruel your touch,
As you whisper of battles, you whisper too much,
Over the bodies of those lost in the fight,
You carry their memories into the night.

Their sacrifice etched in the windswept land,
A testament to courage, a fate so grand,
Yet the sadness lingers, a heavy shroud,
As the cold winds blow, voices cry aloud.

In the quiet of night, their spirits roam,
Seeking solace, seeking a way back home,
But the winds keep on howling, a mournful sound,
Over the battlefield where peace is not found.

So let us remember, in solemn grace,
The lives that were taken in that distant place,
And may the winds one day carry away,
The pain and the sorrow that forever stay.

As The Sun Sets Low

As the sun dips low o'er the seashore's edge,
A solemn moment, we must now pledge,
To remember those lost, the brave and the free,
In the Falklands War, by the vast, unforgiving sea.

Beneath the golden hues of the setting sun,
Courageous hearts fought, their battles begun,
Amidst the waves' fury and the bitter cold,
Their stories of loss, forever told.

In the South Atlantic's tempestuous embrace,
A conflict unfolded in a desolate space,
Sailors and soldiers, their lives on the line,
For their homeland's honour, they did shine.

The sea, a relentless and formidable foe,
Took some from us, where the wild winds blow,
But in our hearts, their memory remains,
Their sacrifice not lost, in history's chains.

Let us not forget those who served with pride,
On both sides of the conflict, on that turbulent tide,
For in remembrance, we find the way,
To honour the fallen, and their bravery display.

As the sun sets low o'er the seashore's crest,
In our thoughts and prayers, they shall forever rest,
The souls who journeyed to the unknown deep,
In the Falklands War, their watch we shall keep.

Chapter 9

A Veteran Reminisces

> *Time heals, but sometimes it doesn't.*
>
> *Until you have seen the things that happen in war, the smells, the sounds, the screams, the silence, the pain, you will never understand what goes through a veterans head. You may see him proudly adorning his medals, having a laugh with other veterans, but you won't see his memories. You won't see that one moment that changed him from boy to man too early, and all the things afterwards that nearly destroyed him.*

I Couldn't Just Tell You.

I couldn't just tell you, not you , my mum,
So the pressure just built up like an exploding bomb.
A youngster I left, heading off to sea,
exploring, excitement all waiting for me.

To where I was going, I didn't really know,
No war was declared we were going for show.
It got warmer and warmer until it got hot,
Us youngsters were loving all the sun we got.

We kept sailing and working our way through the sea,
What an adventure this was turning into for me.
The weather then took a turn for the worse,
Dark clouds and big waves had started their curse.

Then came the news the Captain had said,
We had sunk the Belgrano many men dead.
It didn't stop there our own aircraft lost,
Aircrewmen and SAS paid the ultimate cost.

Ships being bombed not all could flee,
Young men wanting adventure being buried at sea.
On land sea and harbour lessons would be learned,
In the meantime we heard of the men badly burned.

In the mountains the soldiers gave all that they got,
But sadly we lost some, one by one they were shot.
These memories they haunt me, mum I can't lie,
It's not something I can live with It's my time to die.

They Are In My Soul

In shadows cast by time's unyielding hand,
I walk the path of life, a war-worn man,
A veteran, survivor of the fray,
Yet still, the past in memories holds sway.

Each day unfolds, a battle of its own,
But in my heart, the seeds of war are sown.
For when I glimpse the names upon the stone,
Tears fall like rain, and I am not alone.

Inscribed in stone, their stories etched in pain,
I see the faces, I hear their cries again.
The comrades lost, the sacrifices made,
Their memories haunt me, they will never fade.

I strive to carry on, to find my way,
To live a life that's brighter than the grey.
But in the quiet of the darkest night,
The past returns, igniting memories' light.

The camaraderie, the courage, and the fear,
The bonds we forged, the battles we held dear,
They linger in my soul, forever near,
A sacred flame that I will always steer.

So let me weep for all that once was lost,
For those who paid the ultimate cost.
For though I soldier on, my heart does know,
The price of peace, the weight of memories' woe.

Yet in the tears that fall, a healing grace,
A tribute to the warriors we embrace.
For in our grief, we honour and we strive,
To keep their memory, their sacrifice, alive.

In this conflicting dance of past and present,
I find the strength to cherish life's descent.
To honour those who rest in history's care,
And find in love and hope a path to bear.

So though I cry, my tears are not in vain,
For in my heart, their legacy remains.
In every step I take, I shall proclaim,
Their memory lives on in my silent flame.

The War Veteran

He sits and slowly sips his beer,
As he wipes away the occasional tear.
In the dimly lit pub, he finds solace here,
A war veteran, haunted by memories clear.

His eyes, once filled with youthful grace,
Now bear the weight of a battle-scarred face.
Lines etched by time, a silent embrace,
Of a life forever changed in that distant place.

He stares into the distance, lost in thought,
Recalling the battles where so much was sought.
Comrades in arms, the battles they fought,
In the chaos of war, lessons hard-taught.

The echoes of gunfire still ring in his mind,
As he remembers friends, left behind.
In the gulleys and crevices, where they were confined,
He wonders if they ever found peace of a kind.

The pub's chatter fades into the past,
As his memories flood in, a relentless blast.
Faces of friends, whose lives couldn't last,
In the theatre of war, where shadows were cast.

Amid the pain and the loss he endured,
A sense of duty and honour assured.
He served his country, his heart remained stirred,
A war veteran's tale, in each memory preserved.

As he sits and slowly sips his beer,
In the quiet of the pub, a solitary seer,
He remembers the battles, both far and near,
A war veteran's soul, forever sincere.

Though time has passed, the scars remain,
In his heart and mind, where they drive him insane.
A testament to courage, in spite of the pain,
A war veteran's story, a lifelong refrain.

Why Do They Ask?

Why do they ask? The haunting query looms,
A past of pain, a silent war's dark rooms,
I fought in Falklands, where the battles raged,
But to unveil the horrors, I'm not engaged.

The memories, they linger, a heavy burden borne,
Invisible wounds and scars, forever worn,
Each question digs deeper, reopens old wounds,
Yet, they persist, their curiosity balloons.

They seek the stories, the tales untold,
Of battles and horrors, in that land so cold,
Within me lies a world they cannot know,
A battleground of shadows, where nightmares grow.

I bear the weight of what I've seen and done,
But in their quest for knowledge, they've just begun,
To understand the torment etched within my soul,
The agony and anguish, the relentless toll.

Why do they ask, the details to expose,
When they can't comprehend the pain that flows?
I yearn for peace, to heal, to find my way,
So, please, let me carry these memories alone today.

Respect my silence, the choices I have made,
For in the depths of darkness, my demons are laid,
The Falklands war, a chapter I can't forget,
Let me keep its horrors, a secret I regret.

I'd Trade My Medals

In the shadows of our history, we find,
A question that still lingers in my mind,
Why must we fight, in endless, vicious spin,
When peace should be the prize we yearn to win?

A tragic dance of nations, swords unsheathed,
In pursuit of power, vengeance, or greed,
In this relentless circle, we are bound,
As we trample on hallowed, bloodied ground.

Oh, why do we, as human souls, compete,
In battles where the cost is lives so sweet?
Men, women, children, innocence laid bare,
Lost to the horrors that we cannot bear.

The medals that we wear, they gleam with pride,
But tears of sorrow cannot be denied,
For in their shine, a dark and haunting truth,
That medals come at the expense of youth.

I'd trade my medals for a world at peace,
Where pain and suffering find their release,
For in the end, no victory can erase,
The emptiness left in a war's cruel embrace.

Let us not celebrate the spoils of war,
But mourn the lives we've lost, forevermore,
And strive to break the cycle, find our way,
To a world where peace and lives hold sway.

Let me sleep

In the depths of night, where shadows creep,
A sailor's heart, burdened deep,
Touched by battles, a soul does weep,
Yearning for solace, in dreams to keep.

On the ship we sailed, with pride and might,
Amidst the chaos, in the Falklands' fight,
But scars unseen, haunt day and night,
The haunting echoes, refuse to alight.

Oh, let me sleep, in peaceful embrace,
Where nightmares fade, and sorrows erase,
Beneath the moon's soft, tender grace,
Grant respite from this torment's chase.

I close my eyes, seeking refuge in slumber,
Away from the sounds of aircraft going over,
Yet memories surge, as emotions encumber,
Relentless ghosts of war, my mind's plunder.

Let me drift upon gentle seas, calm and serene,
Where waves of tranquillity wash me clean,
Carry me far from the horrors I've seen,
To a haven of dreams, where wounds can convene.

In dreams, let me sail on an endless sea,
Away from the strife that continues to be,
With each gentle sway, let my heart find decree,
Release me from this pain, set my spirit free.

I yearn for peace, where innocence thrives,
Where war-torn thoughts no longer arrive,
In sleep's embrace, let darkness derive,
The soothing balm, my soul shall revive.

Let me sleep, where the stars are my guide,
Through ethereal realms, let my spirit glide,
Grant me respite, on this harrowing tide,
So my restless mind may finally subside.

In the realm of dreams, let me find release,
Where burdens are lifted, and troubles decrease,
For in slumber's embrace, my soul finds peace,
Grant me solace, let the torment cease.

Let me sleep, in a haven so deep,
Where memories fade, and nightmares sleep,
In dreams, let my spirit soar and sweep,
Oh, grant me solace, in dreams let me keep.

It's ok to cry

It's ok to cry, dear veterans bold,
As time spins its tale, forty-one years old.
In shadows of war, your memories reside,
Etched deep in your hearts, where emotions reside.

The aircraft soaring, a thunderous might,
Over Falklands' skies, in the darkest of nights.
The guns' relentless roar, echoing loud,
A symphony of battle, amid the shroud.

Through long yomps you marched, resolute and brave,
Over rugged terrains, your spirits engrave.
The ships that carried you, steadfast and true,
Across treacherous waters, to face what's due.

In those restless nights, with tracer bullets' light,
A haunting display, in the darkness' might.
Through gulleys, you pressed, with courage untamed,
As bullets whizzed by, the world seemed inflamed.

And in the midst of it all, faces you've met,
Lives intertwined, in a war's tragic bet.
Though duty compelled you, to stand and to fight,
The weight of those lost, shadows day and night.

But remember, dear souls, it's ok to feel,
The sorrow, the pain, the wounds that won't heal.
For in tears, there's strength, in vulnerability, might,
And healing begins, with emotions in sight.

You carried a burden, not meant to bear alone,
Reach out to each other, your hearts to atone.
United as one, find solace and care,
In each other's embrace, find strength to repair.

For forty-one years may have passed, it's true,
Yet the memories linger, like morning dew.
Let tears cleanse the wounds, that still remain raw,
As you remember the fallen, with hearts that still draw.

It's ok to cry, dear veterans strong,
Together you stand, and together belong.
In the echoes of history, your bond will endure,
As you remember the days of the Falklands War.

Alone in the Dark

In the silent shadows where memories reside,
Lurk the ghosts of battles, impossible to hide.
Whispers of the past, like chains that bind,
Echoes of the war, forever etched in the mind.

The world sees a smile, but behind closed doors,
The mind replays scenes of relentless wars.
Screams in the night, when all should be calm,
The haunting grip of PTSD's unyielding palm.

Each day is a battle, against demons unseen,
Wounds that won't heal, scars deep and unclean.
The world moves on, but the man stands still,
Trapped in a moment, against their own will.

Faces of fallen comrades, in dreams they appear,
Voices of the lost, ringing loud and clear.
The weight of survivor's guilt, heavy to bear,
A constant reminder, of the price of warfare.

Seeking solace in solitude, away from the light,
For in the darkness, the demons take flight.
But hope is a flame, that can pierce through the night,
Guiding the lost, towards healing and light.

From Boy to Man

In fields where once the children played,
Now lies the stage of war's parade,
A boy, too young, with dreams in hand,
Is called to fight, to take a stand.

From boy to man, the journey's swift,
In trenches deep and fog adrift,
With gun in hand and helmet worn,
He faces night, he faces morn.

The innocence of youth is lost,
Replaced by war's unending cost,
A face once bright with hope and cheer,
Now lined with pain, now lined with fear.

He fights for honour, fights for pride,
With comrades falling by his side,
The battle rages, loud and grim,
The chances of return grow dim.

From boy to man, he's forced to grow,
In fields where blood and sorrow flow,
He learns the price of victory,
The cost of human dignity.

And when the war has reached its end,
He's left to ponder, left to mend,
A man now shaped by war's cruel hand,
A boy no more, in no man's land.

From boy to man, a path so bleak,
A tale of war no tongue can speak,
A lesson learned in pain and strife,
The fragile, fleeting gift of life.

There is a Pint on the Bar

In a dim-lit tavern, where shadows creep,
A pint on the bar, untouched, does weep,
A tale of bravery, a tale of despair,
A pilot's story, a burden to bear.

Once a hero, soaring the skies,
With dreams in his eyes and no compromise,
He danced with the clouds, he kissed the sun,
But war's cruel hand can't be undone.

A battle erupted, a tempest of fire,
A dance with death, a funeral pyre,
He fought with honour, he fought with grace,
But fate had marked its cold embrace.

His plane was struck, a wound so deep,
A fall from the heavens, a plunge so steep,
A cry was heard, a soul was torn,
A hero was lost, a legend was born.

Back at the tavern, where friends would meet,
A pint was poured, a gesture so sweet,
A drink for the fallen, a drink for the brave,
A drink for the pilot, who found his grave.

Days turned to weeks, and weeks to years,
The pint on the bar, a symbol of tears,
A memory of valour, a memory of pain,
A memory of a hero, never to fly again.

In that dim-lit tavern, where shadows creep,
There is a pint on the bar, and it still does weep,
A tale of sorrow, a tale so raw,
A tale of a pilot, killed in war.

So raise your glasses, and let us toast,
To the ones we've lost, the ones we miss most,
For in their memory, we find our way,
In their honour, we live another day.

There is a pint on the bar, and it's waiting still,
A symbol of loss, a void to fill,
A reminder of war, a reminder of cost,
A reminder of all that we've loved and lost.

I Hear the Sounds

Amidst the shadows of the night,
A haunted mind takes its flight,
To distant seas and battles waged,
Upon an aircraft carrier's stage.

In Falklands' bitter, chilling breeze,
A soul endured its dark unease,
Upon that ship, a vessel cold,
Where tales of anguish still unfold.

I hear the sounds, a haunting call,
The echoes of the warlords' brawl,
The distant thunder, guns ablaze,
In memories, a twisted maze.

The deck would tremble 'neath my feet,
As sea harriers roared, their engines beat,
Yet in my heart, a silent scream,
A nightmare's dance, a shattered dream.

Faces lost in ghostly mist,
Comrades fallen, love dismissed,
The cries of wounded souls arise,
A symphony of distant cries.

The waters churned with crimson tides,
As battles raged on all sides,
And in the depths, the secrets keep,
The tears of those who couldn't weep.

I hear the sounds, a mournful dirge,
The pain within, an endless surge,
A fractured mind, a fractured soul,
Invisible wounds that take their toll.

The years have passed, the war is done,
But battles linger, never won,
In quiet moments, shadows creep,
The memories that never sleep.

"I Hear the Sounds," a whispered plea,
For understanding, let it be,
To heal the hearts that bear the weight,
Of scars that time can't mitigate.

In darkness, may the light find way,
To guide the tormented soul astray,
To mend the wounds that lie within,
And grant the chance to live again.

A Veteran Stands

In shadows of a storied past, a veteran stands,
A Royal Marine with weathered hands.
His memory, once sharp as a saber's gleam,
Now drifts in the fog of an Alzheimer's dream.

In youth, he wore the uniform with pride,
With courage as his compass, he marched beside
Comrades in arms, through battles hard-fought,
In lands unknown, where bravery was sought.

But time, relentless, has stolen his grasp,
Like sand slipping through an hourglass's clasp.
His medals gleam dimly on the old fireplace shelf,
As he journeys through the labyrinth of himself.

In forgotten battles, he once fought so bold,
Where tales of bravery and honour were told,
Now lie buried beneath the shroud of his mind,
Like treasures of the past, left far behind.

Yet still, in his eyes, a glimmer remains,
A spark of the warrior, the strength that sustains.
Though memories fade like footprints in the sand,
The heart of a Marine forever will stand.

So let us honour this veteran's grace,
As he sails on through the tides of time's embrace.
In his fading memories, we'll stand by his side,
For a Royal Marine's spirit will never subside.

In the twilight of days, he may not recall,
The battles he fought, the comrades who'd fall,
But we'll cherish the moments, the love that remains,
For a Royal Marine's legacy forever remains.

He was just 18 when Andy Trish found himself thrust into the heart of historic turmoil when news of the Argentinian invasion on South Georgia broke. On a brief respite at home, his leave was abruptly cut short as he received an urgent recall to his ship, HMS Hermes. Within three days, the Falklands Flagship set sail, leaving behind the familiar comforts of home.

Meanwhile, fate had another plan for Andy's family, as his brother David embarked on a journey southward aboard the HMS Antelope. The ominous date of May 23, 1982, forever etched in memory, marked the day when four Argentinian A-4B Skyhawks descended upon HMS Antelope in a harrowing attack. Remarkably, David survived this perilous encounter, emerging from the crucible of war.

This pivotal moment unfolded just a day after Andy's 19th birthday, a stark reminder of the relentless nature of conflict. Andy, with a storyteller's gift, captures the essence of these events, offering a firsthand account that transports the listener into the midst of chaos and the profound pain of war. Whether he channels the voice of a man, woman, child, soldier, or sailor, Andy's narrative prowess immerses you in the visceral experience of those turbulent times.

www.ingramcontent.com/pod-product-compliance
Lightning Source LLC
Chambersburg PA
CBHW071450080526
44587CB00014B/2060